What People are sayin

Magic for Hedge W

With its foundations firmly in creating meaningful connections to nature and beyond, this book feels like a warm welcome into a magical world that many live alongside without even realising it. Harmonia explores folk magic and practices, recommends eco-friendly ways of working, and emphasises the power of using the right ingredients. Any solitary practitioner can take much from these pages, from mindfully choosing to reconnect with trees and plants to seeking the spirit within a stone. I feel like it's never been more vital to take the advice from Harmonia's book, to pause to notice the tiny details in nature, and the everyday magic that imbues our incredible world. Truly a book that helps rekindle the spark of magic in all of us as well as a practical volume and "how to" guide for the aspiring Hedge Witch.

Mabh Savage, author of *Practically Pagan: An Alternative Guide to Planet Friendly Living*

The first thing that struck me was just how much information there is in this book. Full of anecdotes, practical exercises, and information from a range of sources, it is perfect for anyone who is looking for a hands-on approach. Whilst the author herself has described this as a 'short guide or introduction', this book feels like so much more thanks to the wealth of knowledge included. *Magic for Hedge Witches* really does stand out from the rest. And yet despite all the information in this book, it is clear that we are just scratching the surface of the author's knowledge and experience with hedge magic.

One section which really stood out to me was the section on sourcing old spells. Harmonia does a fantastic job of showing us how we can take spells and charms of old and rework them to make them suitable for modern magic without losing any of their connection to their origins. This blending of traditional practices and folklore with the modern is prevalent throughout the book in a way that is genuinely inspiring.

I believe that anyone who feels a connection with the natural world and uses that as a focus for their magic would benefit from this book. It is one I can see myself going back to time after time. As you may have guessed I loved this book, and highly recommend it.

Jessica Howard, author of *Pagan Portals – The Art of Lithomancy*

As someone who works shamanically I am always fascinated by the similarities and differences between the way I work and the way of a Hedge Witch such as Harmonia Saille. This book drew me in immediately and had me hooked completely well before the second chapter. This is not just a book for beginners, despite being under the Pagan Portal's umbrella, but a book that reaches out to everyone who uses 'magic' in their lives and work, Witch or otherwise. The author's personal practice and experience is delightfully interwoven with historical references, practical exercises and suggestions, making it both a guide and a resource for coming back to over and over again.

Yvonne Ryves, Author: *Shaman Pathways – Web of Life*

Hedgewitchery is experiencing a revival within the pagan community and Harmonia Saille is publishing her third captivating title in the Moon Books Pagan Portals series on the subject: Magic for Hedge Witches. It might also be referred to as 'green' or folk-craft because its focus is on the practical side of folk magic which incorporates much in the way of natural ingredients, the elements of nature, and the magic of hedge riding, which the author terms 'hedge magic'. Coming from a highly experienced magical practitioner, there are suggestions on how to source spells and ingredients, and connect them with rituals, practical exercises, useful correspondences, familiars...and not forgetting how to put a spell together from your own recipes, in order to give a good grounding in the rudiments of hedge magic.

As Harmonia says, the practical side of her magical practice is based on folk magic, an uncomplicated magic brewed up by cunning folk and wise-women. "Uncomplicated does not mean "uninteresting" or "requiring little learning" though. Folk magic is a craft taught or self-taught over years and nowadays is often gleaned from or based on the ancient mixed in with modern knowledge or practices." Within traditional British Old Craft it is the lowly level of the 'parish-pump' witch whereby we seek out "natural ingredients along with using natural amulets and making personal connections with them".

Hedge riding helps us take the practice to the next level by entering an altered state of consciousnesses to travel to the Otherworld to contact spirit guides, teachers, and ancestors to seek spiritual guidance on a level that Jung referred to as the collective unconscious.

Harmonia Saille takes us on a journey into the world of the hedge witch so that we can learn to explore these magical practices for ourselves.

Melusine Draco, author of the *'Traditional Witchcraft'* series

Magic for Hedge Witches is a fillerless information-packed handbook for those looking to continue their journey of exploration in hedge magic. Harmonia Saille uses her years of personal application to great impact, passing on decades of research in one handy guide. Harmonia's works are a consistent joy which allow readers to fruitfully add to their voyage through pagan practice. This is a home library must-have which cuts through the treacle and gets the must-know of magic. If you have not had the pleasure of reading this author's other works then this is a brilliant introduction.

Johnnie Maguire, Hedge Witch, Playwright, and Author, *Kitty: Queen of the Washhouse, Weave* and *The Liver Bird*

Pagan Portals

Magic for Hedge Witches

Sourcing Ingredients, Connection,
Spell Building

Pagan Portals

Magic for Hedge Witches

Sourcing Ingredients, Connection,
Spell Building

Harmonia Saille

MOON
BOOKS

Winchester, UK
Washington, USA

JOHN HUNT PUBLISHING

First published by Moon Books, 2022
Moon Books is an imprint of John Hunt Publishing Ltd., No. 3 East Street, Alresford
Hampshire SO24 9EE, UK
office@jhpbooks.net
www.johnhuntpublishing.com
www.moon-books.net

For distributor details and how to order please visit the 'Ordering' section on our website.

Text copyright: Harmonia Saille 2021

ISBN: 978 1 78099 421 5
978 1 78099 422 2 (ebook)
Library of Congress Control Number: 2021939166

Design: Matthew Greenfield

UK: Printed and bound by CPI Group (UK) Ltd, Croydon, CR0 4YY
Printed in North America by CPI GPS partners

We operate a distinctive and ethical publishing philosophy in
all areas of our business, from our global network of authors to
production and worldwide distribution.

Contents

For Lauri Lee and all my readers with many thanks.

Preface

Magic is a significant part of my personal pathway. When I think of magic as a hedge-riding hedge witch, I think of the forests, mountains, fields, plains, and rivers and seas. Magic is within nature and I bring nature into my personal magical practices whether I am collecting twigs, leaves, pebbles, glass and more, or in hedge riding where I travel the forests and mountains of the other realms searching for answers to everyday problems. In hedge riding I use magic in conjunction with divination and healing, but my general magical practices are eclectic and rooted in folk magic.

Folk magic has on occasion been labeled "primitive" as if it has no value. Needless to say, those of us who practice folk magic know that it does. Regarding intent, what you put into it is what you get out of it, and folk magic can yield the same results as ceremonial magic. In addition, even the simplest of spells can have a breadth of knowledge behind it.

Whichever type of magic you practice, it requires a period of learning; it is not something you achieve overnight. Magical training, in fact, can be compared to an apprenticeship – intense study and practice. This is often self-taught, in that competency in skills is built up over time, more often years. There will certainly be reading involved. Strengthening your intuition is another important element. Learning about your ingredients, their qualities and purpose, and connecting to them is another. All this will help you become more competent in practicing magic.

Magic is experiential, so you do need to practice and, over time, develop the proficiency you need for it to be effective. However, it does not end there. Your magical training and education are ongoing – always seeking, always learning new skills.

I am a hedge witch and hedge witches are by nature solitary and their individual paths vary. It is difficult therefore to tailor a book to suit all hedge witches or, indeed, solitary witches on any pathway. However, I have based the practical side of this book on folk magic which incorporates much in the way of natural ingredients and elements of nature, and magic in hedge riding. Together I term them "hedge magic." This is the third book in the Hedge Witch series following on from the *Pagan Portals* guides *Hedge Witchcraft* and *Hedge Riding*.

If you are a hedge witch interested in magic and at the start of that journey, or a curious green, hearth, kitchen witch, or anyone interested in magic, then I hope that you will find something of use. All I can do within my books is to share my own magical experiences and practices gained over twenty-seven years and during more than two decades as a hedge witch.

My approach in this book is to demonstrate the processes I go through in using magic and creating spells. You will find suggestions on how to source spells, how to source ingredients and connect with them, ritual, practical exercises, useful correspondences, familiars, and how to put a spell together from your own recipes, so that you have a good grounding in the rudiments of hedge magic. For hedge witches, the last section is how to use magic in hedge riding.

There are many books written about magic and some of the content of this book will correspond with those. However, I hope you also find something new here and aspects of working with magic you have not previously explored.

A big thank you goes to everyone at John Hunt Publishing and Moon Books as well as my family and friends who supported me during the writing and publishing of this guide.

Harmonia Saille

The Rudiments of Hedge Magic

What is Hedge Magic?

My personal magical practice is a blend of folk magic and magic within hedge riding. The two together I term as "hedge magic." Magic in hedge riding can be useful in helping you to decide the core of a problem and what type of spell to use to correct it. A hedge riding journey can also reveal to you what other elements you might add to your spell to enhance it and for help in resolving your dilemmas.

The practical side of my magical practice is based on folk magic. Folk magic is an uncomplicated magic brewed up by cunning folk, the witch, or others. Uncomplicated does not mean "uninteresting" or "requiring little learning" though. Folk magic is a craft taught or self-taught over years and nowadays is often gleaned from or based on the ancient mixed in with modern knowledge or practices.

In past times, superstitions, spells, and charms were passed down not through secret covens of witches but through the ordinary population and almost certainly by way of the cunning man or woman. Folk magic was magical practice for the ordinary folk. This is demonstrated below.

King James I (King James VI of Scotland) as the character Philomathes wrote in his book *Daemonolgie* (Book I, Chapter V, 1597):

> But how prooue ye now that these charmes or vnnaturall practicques are vnlawfull: For so, many honest & merrie men & women haue publicklie practized some of them, that I thinke if ye would accuse them al of Witch-craft, ye would affirme more nor ye will be beleeued in.

The Early Modern English text is difficult to understand but roughly translated it asks – how can you prove that witchcraft is unnatural and unlawful when so many ordinary men and women openly practice it? In writing *Daemonolgie*, King James sought to argue "logically" that anyone who practiced witchcraft, in his opinion, worked with the devil. The discourse between his two characters, the skeptical Philomathes and the supporter Epistemon, he believed would prove among other things that practitioners of all forms of magic were linked to the devil.

Needless to say, he supported witch-hunts, though as the prosecutions increased and got out of hand he later "...revoked the standing commissions against witchcraft."[1]

However, to return to the subject of magic and the common folk, we learn something from this discourse. When King James writes about how many "honest" and "merrie" men and women publicly used charms, he confirms that in fact using charms was common within the population. He also puts forward that many more women than men practiced magic (in his opinion because they were weaker and more susceptible to the devil's influence). In reality, women would have been likely to include healing and herbal medicines as part of their household skills, some of which were quasi-magical.[2]

A cure for an illness for instance might involve healing herbs but also a charm. During those times, people naturally became more careful in using folk magic for fear of being prosecuted, but the practice did continue over the following centuries even if perhaps not as openly. The people who did practice might not have considered themselves to be witches or consider what they did necessarily to be witchcraft. Healing and magic were more often seen as one.

Even among the educated, a good example of someone mixing medicine and the occult is 17th-century herbalist Nicholas Culpeper, who combined astrology with herbal medicine (more about Culpeper in the chapter on "Ingredients"). Often called the father of contemporary medicine, he did offer free services to the general public. He was tried and acquitted of witchcraft in 1642, during the reign of Charles I. Unfortunately, he died young, at 37, from tuberculosis. His legacy remains with us in his recordings of herbs and their uses. His book *Culpeper's Complete Herbal* is still available to buy. I bought my Wordsworth Edition cheaply from a small bookshop in the 90s.

Nowadays, we are lucky in the West that we can openly practice magic. Practitioners might call themselves witches or may follow another pathway that involves the practice of magic or might consider themselves a practitioner of magic without a set pathway. You still do not have to be a witch to use a charm. People often use charms without realizing it. Turning over a silver coin on the new moon is a charm, as is the sprig of heather you bought for luck from a gypsy and wearing the angel pendant that someone bought you to wear for protection or healing.

When we practice folk magic, we are drawing from an age-old tradition. Just like in past times, we do not need a lot of expensive equipment though that is entirely up to the practitioner. For those on a budget or those who prefer to use recycled or natural items, supplies can be built up to great satisfaction. You might though wish to purchase a few items such as charcoal for burning incense, herbs if you do not have the facilities to grow them yourself, and candles (I recommend beeswax, which now come in a variety of colors. You can also make your own). Expenses are also likely to be incurred buying reference books. However, you can make use of items you already have too – dishes, candle holders, knives for cutting and so forth.

Where possible (regarding ingredients) items of biodegradable material should be found and used, so that at some point they become part of the natural earth rather than lying around for centuries littering it. There is something gratifying in seeking out and finding natural ingredients along with using natural amulets and making personal connections with them. This will bring about more satisfying, effective, and powerful magical results.

In modern times, too many things are done for us for convenience. Purchasing complete magical spells that you have not put together yourself defeats the object of crafting. I cannot imagine buying a magical herb mix and not knowing what was in it and what qualities the individual herbs are bringing to the mix. Furthermore, you do not know what someone had in mind when they put it together. But I am sure others have no problem with this for many reasons. However, in creating your magic from scratch, you will find that it is not only an enjoyable experience, but you are increasing your magical knowledge and are becoming a more competent practitioner. Therefore, it is well worth reserving some time, even if it is only at weekends, to gather ingredients and study and research items you find or intend to use. Making connections with them will enhance your magic.

Connection

Learning to Connect with Your Ingredients

Before we move on to sourcing old spells and ingredients in general, a discussion worth having is that of connection. I hope this section sheds some light on how connecting to items and ingredients within your magical practice can enhance the power of the spell or charm you create. Learning to connect is a skill worth putting time into when first embarking on your magical apprenticeship. It may well lead you to a different choice of ingredients than you have ever considered before.

Connection is important in any magic. Perhaps I do rather go on about this as connecting to everything within nature along with nature spirits is important to me personally. Those who practice nature-based magic will often make connections with the plants, herbs, and flowers that they use within it. However, it is not just living plants that they do this with but also other items they may use in their magical practice such as water, rocks, bark, fir cones, twigs, smooth broken glass, soil or sand, and shells. If you view them as animate – like animals – then you will understand what I mean. I do not mean by this that when you use a stone, incense, or an herb you empower it for your magical work, though you can do this, but you connect also with its natural spiritual essence.

Some witches find it easier to connect with objects than others. They might well be psychic, empathic, or sensitive in some way and can feel or even see energy emanating from the plant or stone. But not everyone can connect with objects so easily. However, with practice, you can improve your connections and strengthen your instinct, becoming more sensitive to other living beings whether it be animals or plant life or inanimate objects such as stones and shells.

The hedge between the worlds is not a boundary, but a veil, and at certain times of the day and year that veil thins, and beings from the other world can more easily pass into ours. The human world is connected with the spirit world, and we are all related to each other. Everything is connected: not just the flora and fauna, but also what might appear as inanimate. We are connected to the earth beneath our feet, the wind, rain, and sun, the elements, the moon, and even the outer universe. To connect you need to avoid building barriers in your head and open yourself up to these wonderful relationships.

The material world reigns supreme with all the consumerism that goes with it. A material world that separates you from nature. But if you consciously tune in, observe, see the landscape around you and all that it contains, get to know it, you can close that gap between you. In our normal lives, we might take a trip to the countryside, enjoy it, and might picnic or walk. You might feel calm and that is why you go out to the countryside or into the wild, to get away from it all (everyday life), and that is the first step to making deeper connections. To make further connections we need to *feel* it – view what we see as alive and sentient.

Wild and Domesticated

Even in the city, wildness is everywhere. We make connections with our partner, children, friends, and family. It comes easily to us. However, connecting with the wildness often takes effort as we no longer do this naturally. As I have said above as time has passed, humankind has turned away from nature, becoming separate from it, losing its meaning. I mention in my book *Hedge Witchcraft* that there is more to nature than seeing it as something to control and master. We should be aware of it, to stop, and appreciate seeing the spider in the web, or the leaf falling from the tree, the bluebell forcing its way through the soil in the garden or in the hedgerow, hear the bird singing the morning chorus, or the wind whistling through the trees. We should make time to see things around us, the land around us, to be aware, to stop objectifying things, seeing them as inert. Be present, tune in, and create a symbiotic relationship with the natural world. If we keep doing this it comes more naturally to us. All of us, the animals, insects, plants, water, wind, mountains, forests, land, we are one. We are all connected – part of the cycle of birth, life, death, and rebirth. It is not just connecting with everything; it is letting it – allowing it – to connect with us. It is a relationship – the feeling and exchanging of energy. Sensing the consciousness of everything around you.

Just to begin to relate to nature around us is a good start. Open your senses including your sixth sense. Look around you. See what is in the immediate vicinity. Not just the bigger things – the mountains, rivers, forests, even the wind, but the smaller ones – the leaf, the wildflower, the pebble. Pick something up – touch it, listen to it, converse with it, smell it and, most of all, sense it, accept it, and feel it within you. Listen too. Hear the insects buzzing, the running water of the tiny stream, animals foraging in the undergrowth.

You can form those relationships in different ways, you might intuit, hear, smell, recognize, see, or touch different objects. Everyone is different and we make connections to suit. For example, we might automatically want to put our hand in the stream and feel the water run over our fingers; touch the velvet of the leaf or petal; feel the breeze on our faces, the rain on our skin; and sense or even see the energy from the pebble or tree. You might make such a connection with a particular tree, say a birch or aspen, as I have. You might instantly recognize the old oak, the guardian tree, a symbol of strength, and a harbinger of change. The dryad guardian spirit is attached to oaks. You might stop and converse with her, and occasionally request help. You might see a heron as a carrier of spirit messages, the floating white feather as a message from a deceased loved one, or the bee as an otherworld messenger, and they appear to draw your eye to them.

Often, we find it easier to connect to things outside our world, the universe: planets, the Sun, and the Moon in particular. We speak to her, let her connect with us, and we practice our magic with her, following her phases. We might also connect with Mother Nature and the seasons in the same way. However, we often do not look at individual things – what seems to be insignificant next to the magnificent.

We can, in essence, connect with everything that we use within our magical practice. When you engage with a plant for instance, it will help you more in your magical work. You need to feel the spiritual powers and qualities of the plant: not just the traditional qualities such as you might find in Culpeper's book, but also the color, shape, and scent. We often know that a plant is good for this ailment or that. But the look of the plant gives more of the spiritual side of it, and this can be useful in spell work. The shape of it might remind you of something, the pattern on it or even the size. The color might indicate mood. The scent might attract many bees or butterflies and might indicate that it is a lucky plant. Consequently, you can use your eyes and intuition as well as consulting books.

So, is it necessary to be an animist to practice magic? No, but in my opinion, it can make your experience richer, and it can make your magic that much stronger.

I know from living in a farmhouse in rural Ireland in the middle of a forest, half a mile from the nearest house, with only nature to keep me company (and my husband and pets) that you automatically make better connections with nature. There is not much else to make a connection with. So my days (in between working as I do from home), were taken up with collecting kindling, following deer tracks, looking out for the hare and pheasant in the morning, connecting with the many horses in the fields next to the house, walking down to the river and streams that ran through the land, collecting elderflowers and berries, going to the large tree stump each morning that I used as an outdoor altar, and connecting with nature spirits.

I was saturated with connections, thrust into it, immersed. However, you will be surprised how quickly you can lose that total experience as it dumbs down when you live in a village, town or city and you go with the flow of building relationships with people around you and become caught up in it and find it harder to make the same time to go out and bond with everything around you that is non-human.

Everything is subjective. We view, connect, and experience things in our own way. It is up to us as individuals, as a witch often on a solitary path, to find that way. These are purely suggestions, a guide. I am not laying down tenets here – a "you must" do it this way or that.

As a hedge witch myself I reiterate that there are hedge witches of many individual pathways. Still, it is hard to practice any pagan pathway without some connection to nature. In addition, if you look at the world of shamans (of indigenous peoples), then there is always a strong connection with nature and animism as there is with hedge riding.

My own reasoning is that the "hedge" in hedge witchcraft denotes the boundary between the worlds but, at the same time, symbolizes that hedge at the edge of the village, which separates us from the community, putting him or her firmly in the realms of nature.

Your magic will be more successful too if you can remove the barriers you have built up separating you from nature and subsequently become closer to what is around you. Really "seeing" it and "sensing" it. In other words, venture over the hedge.

Connection Exercise 1

- To make connections, begin with a living thing you like to look at, such as a tree. Visit it regularly. Feel the energy coming from it and mingling with your own. Talk to the tree (you can do this psychically). Converse with its spirit. What does it say to you?

- Follow this up by doing the same thing with a plant. This might be fern in the forest, rosemary in your garden, or basil in your window box. Connect with it. What does it say to you? What do you say to it?
- After connecting with living things such as a tree and plant, move on to what you might view as an inanimate object, like a pebble. Pick it up and handle it. Feel the energy. What images do you get when you close your eyes?
- Move onto something you might use regularly in your magic, such as a rune (made from pebbles, metal, or wood) or a crystal. Ignore any traditional meaning of that rune or crystal. What does it say to you, the shape, or the feel? You might find it communicates with you. What do you sense it would be helpful with?

It is what the plant or object is saying to you, that you use within your magic. It is not just connecting with the traditional qualities that are associated with that object, what you have read in a book, but what it means to you personally – spiritually.

Currently, I live in the UK on the edge of a small town close to the Cotswolds by the River Severn. There is a fairly busy road nearby, so the area is by no means as rural as when we lived in Ireland. Luckily, it is still semi-rural and today on my walk by the Severn, I picked up a pebble sparkling with colors that attracted my attention. Additionally, owing to fully focusing, I heard or saw the following things:

- The rustle of the trees in the strong breeze (willow, oak, birch, elder, beech).
- Comfrey, nettle, and thistle.
- Bees and dragonflies.

- A large horse fly (we must take the rough with the smooth).
- Large fish swimming in the marina (possibly roach).
- Two red kites flying overhead and several squawking magpies.
- The feel of the grass underneath my fingers when I sat down for a rest.
- Clouds in the shape of birds and fish.
- Perhaps the most wonderful sighting was a small young deer which ran across the path in front of me from the direction of the river. I did not know there were deer in the immediate area although I have seen foxes, rabbits, badgers, and pheasants.

Try to find a local green space or even public gardens or other people's gardens to regularly visit. Every time you go, try to spot something new. Make notes of the things you do see. You will be surprised at the number of things you have not noticed before.

In doing this you will also begin to notice and find small items and plants to use in your magical workings.

Below is a pathworking exercise to determine the future use of the items you find on your walks in nature.

Connection Exercise 2

- Bring the object home with you if you find it outdoors. You could do the exercise with items you find in your home too. However, switch your pathworking (visualization) session from being outdoors to one involving a castle, or a cave, or somewhere else where you are indoors.
- Make time for your session when you feel relaxed and are unlikely to be disturbed. Use meditation music if you wish for this. Hold the item while you journey.
- Use relaxation techniques as you would to meditate.

Fully relax the body and breathe steadily.

- Presuming you found your item out in nature, this pathworking will involve a walk and a place where you can sit and rest for a while before returning to the starting point.

- Plan your route before you start (set the scene). Start from your own door in your mind but when you open it you will be at the place you have chosen to walk. If your object came from the forest, then let your walk be through a forest too.

- When you are ready, set off on your journey and walking slowly let yourself observe your surroundings. Once you have walked a while, find somewhere to rest and to observe what is around you. If you have walked in a wood or forest, then sit on a log in a copse or grove, or on a rock by a waterfall or river. If you found your item on the beach, then let your journey be along the beach, and when you rest, sit on the sand, sand dune, or on a rock. If in a cave and there is nowhere to sit, then sit down on the ground. Stay for a little while and take note of everything and everybody you see. Does anyone or anything appear? Look for the symbolism. Even note changes in the weather. Remember to listen for sounds.

- After a while return home. Take your time coming back into reality. You may find you had entered into an altered state of consciousness. If you did not, then you should have still gained something from the pathworking.

- Write down everything you saw and heard, even if it seemed insignificant at the time. Do this immediately. If you do not you will be surprised how hard it becomes to recall details later.

- Lastly, divine your results. Does anything stand out? Did you see a bright beam of sunshine? Or an animal? What do they mean to you in the first instance? Try to decipher the symbolism. Use a symbolism book if you need to, but your own instincts as to the significance will be more meaningful. Can you connect any of what you saw or heard with your object? How would that enhance your magical practice (in what type of spell would it be useful?). Remember to label the item to distinguish it from others that might look similar. Or keep it with other items that you use for the same magical purpose.

• You can also sleep with the item under your pillow to see what your dreams reveal. Do this the same day as the pathworking if possible.

Magical Stones

Stones hold a particular fascination for me. There is something inherently magical about them. Many witches purify and then empower objects they use within their magic, imbuing them with their own magical qualities. They enhance the natural power within. It is, of course, up to the individual witch whether they do this or not and it is indeed a standard magical practice. However, I once read a comment from a practitioner of magic that an object is only powerful because we make it so. I thought it a shame that the practitioner thought this and was missing out on the connection that you can make with the natural power within it. Stones immediately sprang to mind. This had me immediately reaching for my rather battered copy of *Man and His Symbols*. This book was edited by Carl G. Jung, and he and a number of collaborators contributed to it.

Here we will look at just a few comments on what Jung and others say on stones and natural power. Stones have such valuable use within magical practice they deserve a little more said about them.

In section three of Man and His Symbols "The process of individuation" M.-L. von Franz discusses how rubbing stones is an ancient activity of man. He even points out that Australian aborigines believe that their dead ancestors exist in stones and that by rubbing them, the power increases. Franz says:

> The mathematically precise arrangement of the crystal evokes in us the intuitive feeling that even in so-called "dead" matter there is a spiritual ordering principle at work. Thus, the crystal often symbolically stands for the union of extreme opposites—of matter and spirit.

Franz goes on to say:

> Many people cannot refrain from picking up stones of a slightly unusual color or shape and keeping them, without knowing why they do this. It is as if the stones held a mystery that fascinates them. Men have collected stones since the beginning of time and have apparently assumed that certain ones were the containers of the life-force with all its mystery... For while the human being is as different as possible from a stone, yet man's innermost center is in a strange and special way akin to it.

In his book *Memories, Dreams, Reflections* Carl G. Jung talks about a stone he used as a "life-force" for a manikin he made as a child and was reminded of as an adult.

> Ultimately, the manikin was a kabir, wrapped in his little cloak, hidden in the kista, and provided with a supply of life-force, the oblong black stone.
> (*Chapter I, First Years*)

Jung also writes in the same book:

> Every stone, every plant, every single thing seemed alive and indescribably marvelous. I immersed myself in nature,

crawled, as it were, into the very essence of nature and away from the whole human world.

(*Chapter II, School Years*)

He continues to talk about stones throughout the book:

This impression was reinforced when I became acquainted with Gothic cathedrals. But there the infinity of the cosmos, the chaos of meaning and meaninglessness, of impersonal purpose and mechanical law, were wrapped in stone. This contained and at the same time was the bottomless mystery of being, the embodiment of spirit. What I dimly felt to be my kinship with stone was the divine nature in both, in the dead and the living matter.

(*Chapter II, School Years*)

Additionally, in his book *Memories, Dreams, Reflections* Jung talks of building a wall in his garden. A cornerstone was the wrong size, and a square block had been sent. The Mason was furious and told the barge men to take it back. However, when Jung saw it, he said that it was his stone, and he must have it. He was reminded of a Latin verse by the alchemist, Arnaldus de Villanova. He chiseled it into the stone.

Here stands the mean, uncomely stone,
'Ts very cheap in price!
The more it is despised by fools,
The more loved by the wise.
(*Chapter VIII, The Tower*)

Loved by the wise as stone circles are loved by so many. I was lucky enough to live close to both Stonehenge and Avebury stone circles in Wiltshire for a number of years. I preferred Avebury the largest stone circle in the world as you could freely walk among the stones and I have only done this at Stonehenge at the Summer Solstice. If you visit Avebury off tourist season and in the winter, there are few people milling about and you can better absorb the energies there and hold rituals, or practice magic in one of the fields. I have officiated at a handfasting there. The added joy, just a mile walk away, is Silbury Hill, the great burial mound where you can feel the Otherworld and healing energies. You can no longer get too close as it is protected. Wiltshire has a wealth of burial mounds and henges with major ley lines running across the landscape. You can feel the magical energy there and I found it similar to the magic I felt when living in Ireland. This was also true of the Drombeg stone circle (The Druid's Altar) at beautiful Glandore in County Cork, Ireland, another place better to visit off season. Just sitting on the bank and meditating, absorbing the energy is quite an experience. The Rollright Stones made up of the King's Men Stone Circle, The King Stone, and the Whispering Knights, are not too far from where I live now and are next on my list for a visit. Like many people, I am drawn to stone circles and burial mounds. Stone circles hold mystery. If you are able to spend time at one in quiet contemplation, the energies are healing to the mind and body.

From this section you might gather that stones have a wonderful natural magic. Healing is one of the magical qualities associated with them. I think it is a shame not to connect with the natural and spiritual power of an object even if we do go on to empower it further. As a practitioner of magic, I believe connections are important and it is useful to believe in the oneness of nature and not be above it.

Choosing Objects from Nature

How do we go about finding and choosing magical objects found in nature? A stone can look just like any other stone. However, even a stone that looks unremarkable might have more meaning than you supposed. For instance, consider what attracted you to the stone. Did it sparkle in the light as the sun shone on it? How did you feel at that moment? Was it the shape or the texture? How did it feel when you picked it up and touched it? Perhaps it made you feel good. Perhaps you kept it for good luck. If so, you could use it in spells and charms to attract good luck. If you like the idea of empowering your stone, you might draw or carve a rune into it – Sowilo (Sun) or the image of a sun or another symbol to remind you about the qualities you noticed in it. In doing so you are doing what Franz said is an ancient activity of man and that by (in his words) "rubbing" it or indeed by drawing or carving a symbol on it, you are enhancing the natural power.

We can apply the same process to a twig or branch you find. A few years ago, in the Netherlands, I would love walking up a lane lined with downy birch and willow trees. The birch grew in a line one after the other. One day I was horrified that several had been cut down and relieved that some remained. However, a day or two later the remainder had gone. Needless to say, I was extremely upset about this. I saw branches on the ground and collected two to use as wands. I still have them. I know they are birch so have not carved or written on them. I am glad to say that also, a few days later, I walked up the same lane and heard the singing of a tree tinkling in the breeze. I recognized the sound and looked up and saw one birch tree remaining in among the willows and collected some twigs from around it to use in spells. I do find most types of birch to have magical qualities.

Birch is a noble and sacred tree. In past times, and indeed is still used by witches, it helps sweep out the old year (and welcomes the new). It represents new beginnings and new dawns. The birch has protective qualities (particularly of children) and owing to its white bark also of purification. You jump the birch broom in a handfasting. Often related to the moon, the maiden, Brigid, and spring, it is seen as fertile and feminine. As a rune,

Berkano (Birch) represents new beginnings. I often refer to it as the "baby" rune as it sometimes appears when a pregnancy is forecast, but that could equally be a new start or new project – something in its infancy. In the Ogham divination system based on the Ogham alphabet, birch (beithe, beith, beth) has a similar meaning as the other interpretations here. Color-wise, white associates well with birch (purification, reflection, birth). The color green would work with fertility and growth. Yellow for spring and new beginnings.

When you choose an item from nature for magical use, try to sense the qualities within it, then concentrate on them while thinking of your purpose. If you have collected the item to draw or carve symbols on, then first make your connections to ensure that the magical symbols you intend to draw on it do correspond. Witches often use crystals* for healing and magical work. They find it easy to connect with them. With effort, you can connect in the same way with other items you use within your magic.

*Responsibly sourced crystals are available to buy, which include traceability certificates.

On Sourcing Old Spells

Researching old books is an interesting way to seek out charms of old and then adapt them to fit. We would not always choose to cast spells written centuries ago exactly as they are because those spells were put together for the times those people lived in and they were very different than the way with live now and what we might feel is ethical and right.

Past times are often said to be times of "deep superstition." Superstition has been termed in modern terms by religious bodies as "ignorance," the belief of invisible forces that leads to a *false* interpretation of *natural* happenings – happenings that are also physical and *not* supernatural. Included in this interpretation are charms and spells, astrology, divination, dream analysis, and practices such as walking under ladders, lucky charms, avoiding treading on cracks in the pavement – a wide range of practices.

As a witch or psychic, you might understandably take exception to the terms *"false* interpretation of *natural* happenings" and "physical *not* supernatural." Who is to say that interpretations are *false*, who is to say that happenings are physical and not *supernatural*? If you are experiencing such a happening, it would be hard to convince you that it was not true. An example would be a person who was previously a sceptic seeing a ghost, or in my own case, no one need tell me that when I lived in a house in the forest in Tipperary that what I saw on two separate occasions inches in front my face, were not fairies or nature spirits. I saw them; nothing can explain them away as being physical – so I simply believe. Many things cannot simply be so easily explained away (though people do try to do this – optical illusion, trick of the light – when the event you saw could not possibly be either).

Many years ago, my second youngest son and I saw his doppelganger. He was twelve years old. One evening I had already said goodnight to the family who were watching a film in the sitting room. As I passed my sons' bedroom, I saw the son in question standing in the doorway, wearing his school shirt and socks but no trousers. I was walking quickly, but on seeing him I took a few steps backwards to give him a kiss, but the room was empty. I thought it odd and when I walked on, I could clearly hear his voice coming from the sitting room. Spooked, my stomach turned over, but I did not say anything at that point. The next evening the same son ran into the sitting room scared out of his wits. He had walked past his bedroom and saw a boy sitting on his bed in a school shirt with no trousers on and putting on socks. When he looked again, he was not there. He added, "The worst thing was he looked just like me." A day later when he went to the loo he came out and told me that his urine was "dark." He had mentioned it before, and I had suggested he was dehydrated. But this time, because of what we had both seen, I asked to look and immediately realized this was something more serious. After calling the doctor and him seeing my son right away he was admitted to hospital where he remained for a week having tests for an autoimmune kidney condition. The absence of trousers we had both seen on his doppelganger was a clue to that by emphasizing the lower part of his body. We never saw the doppelganger* again.

*A doppelganger is often seen as a bad omen portending imminent death. Though in this case I would say it was a warning of illness. The house we lived in was built in old hospital grounds and my youngest son who was seven years old often saw spirits of patients (he still does see spirits in adulthood).

Even the most skeptical person would not find it hard to "believe" that if this happened to them there was something more – something spiritual or supernatural. Belief is not so much a general term that can be lumped under one term of "superstition" but something that is personal to the individual.

Often people who castigate others for their beliefs, themselves believe in a god that no one has ever seen but they cannot see the irony in that.

When we practice magic, we believe and trust in a force of Will that will cause changes in our lives and those of others through natural or supernatural forces. The power of belief influences the power of Will. We put time and effort into the intent of spell work and believe in it.

In past times, people also believed in the magic they practiced, though sceptics were around even then. Charms will have been handed down, passed around in the community, or be put together by the practitioner to suit the subject, much as we would now.

Ancient texts have a wealth of useful magical information. However, in researching these old texts for charms, you will need to be discerning and bear in mind the times in which they were written.

One such text in which you may find charms, spells, and healings, many of which do not need adapting to suit our more modern times, is *The Discoverie of Witchcraft* by Reginald Scot (c.1584). Scot wrote the book as an attack on the belief in witchcraft and in doing so wrote about the spells and practices of the general population creating an insight into the witchcraft of the day. King James I (James VI of Scotland) had every copy of this book burned that could be found. To say there was no such thing as witchcraft was a threat to the King's own work on the subject.

This charm from the book is one that could easily be used today:

Item, hang a stone over the afflicted persons bed, which stone hath naturally such a hole in it, as wherein a string may be put through it, and so be hanged over the diseased or bewitched party: be it man, woman, or horse.

The charm above uses what we call a hag stone, and is a simple remedy for possession, bewitchment, or ill health and suits both human and animal. A hag stone is a stone with a hole through it often found in rivers and on beaches. I have several I found on my local beach when I lived in Ireland. It can be a fun and pleasant experience wandering the beach and shallow rivers searching for hag stones. This charm does not need to be adapted in any way. You can tie a piece of string or ribbon through the center of the stone and hang it above the bed of the person who is ill or feels plagued by bad luck. Keep it for this purpose.

Hag stones are often used for health charms. In the Museum of Witchcraft in Boscastle, Cornwall an exhibition included one coupled with a penny and red thread. Other hag-stone charms for good luck would include a key. Keys were also used for protection and hung with the hag stone above doors. You will find various old charms in museums that will provide ideas for spells, so look out for them. Visit a witchcraft museum if you get the chance.

You will find other charms in *The Discoverie of Witchcraft*, particularly in Book Twelve, though digging them out and deciphering is hard work. This is a good one for curing a headache in Chapter XIV:

Tie a halter about your head, wherewith one hath been hanged.

Then again…maybe not! This is where discernment needs to be employed. Hanging is out of fashion and rather gruesome. Nor would I be fussy on putting a noose around my head. Clearly, we need to pick and choose or adapt where necessary.

In Book Twelve of the same book, Scott has this chant which he says is "Another charme that witches use at the gathering of their medicinable herbs."

Haile be thou holy herbe
Growing on the ground,

All in the mount Calvarie*
First wert thou found,
Thou art good for many a sore,
And healest many a wound,
In the name of sweet Iesus**
I take thee from the ground.

*Mount Calvary
**Jesus

Chants and spells were often Christian in nature. To make this chant pagan friendly for the gathering of healing herbs you can change it thus:

Hail be, oh, holy herb
Growing in the ground,
And hail the sacred place
Where first you were found.
You are good for many a sore,
And for healing many a wound.
In the name of Mother Nature,
With thanks, I take you from the ground.

N.B. There are many rules and regulations in the UK and perhaps other countries around picking wildflowers, such as you need the landowner's permission to uproot them. Picking flowers on nature reserves is generally against the law as is picking rare and protected species. Do check first.

There are ancient grimoires from which spells can also be taken. These do tend to contain many negative magic spells. One such text, a mixture of negative and positive magic, is the *Galdrabók* an Icelandic grimoire dated to c.1600, so written around the same time as *The Discoverie of Witchcraft*. It contains 47 spells and staves (runic). You can find lots of information about this online, however Stephen Flowers wrote a book in 1989 *The Galdrabók: An Icelandic Book of Magic* with all the information and diagrams. Secondhand copies are available to buy. There are luck and protection staves, which would need no adapting. I also found the spells "How to Reveal a Thief" (though Reginald Scot in *The Discoverie of Witchcraft* also has several of these), "How to Cause Fear in an Enemy" and "To Win the Love of a Person." (Personal ethics would apply for the last two. Both causing fear in an enemy and making them suffer, and forcing someone to love you, would be termed negative magic if you were trying to avoid it.)

I personally only practice positive magic, though I have experimented in the past with gray areas, but whether a witch practices black, white, or gray magic, is up to the individual. I now only use positive magic to counteract the negative. I do believe there is some sort of return for any negative energy you send out and this guides me. (More on "ethics" later in the book.)

Ingredients

To create spells, apart from intent, we use ingredients. How much you want to learn about them and how fast will depend on skill, knowledge, and general interest. The novice magical practitioner might want to keep spells as simple as possible and develop knowledge over time. That is fine. Where magic is concerned, running before you can walk is ill-advised. You may trip or overwhelm yourself.

General ingredients can be a variety of items, often found in the household, garden, and out in nature. In this case, developing a basic knowledge of herbs would be useful. Herbs along with candles will form the basis of many spells.

Again, I recommend Culpeper's *Complete Herbal*. This is a handy reference also to herbs, their healing properties and provenance (though I suggest it should not be the only book). Nicolas Culpeper was born in 1616, and many herbs within the book would have been deemed safe then, though not necessarily now. However, many are still used in common medicines or have medicines based on them. Culpeper was a physician, apothecary, and astrologist. He said in the original epistle to the book:

> I consulted with my two brothers, DR. REASON and DR. EXPERIENCE, and took a voyage to visit my mother NATURE, by whose advice, together with the help of Dr. DILIGENCE, I at last obtained my desire; and, being warned by MR. HONESTY, a stranger in our days, to publish it to the world, I have done it.
>
> (*Culpeper's Complete Herbal*, Wordsworth Editions Ltd, 1995.)

As well as including herbs and their qualities, Culpeper incorporates astrology into his work. You do not have to. I do occasionally. Astrology, in any form of magic, can be used in different ways from basic to more complicated. For simple magic, if used, it is generally in a more rudimentary fashion. However, when using astrology in magic even in a basic way, we still recognize there is a whole science behind it. The same reasoning often applies to even the simplest of herbs we often never give a second thought to apart from in cooking or hanging at Yule. There is often a rich and magical folklore behind each one.

I would advise buying several books that not only give the healing property of herbs but the folklore and magical properties. A good encyclopedia of herbs will do this. You can find lots of information online, but read widely. They will help you determine if an herb is suitable for the spell you intend to create.

Books on herbs do not have to be written by pagans. However, pagans do write herbal reference books too. I have the general *Pocket Encyclopedia of Herbs* edited by Lesley Bremness which I bought many years ago. Another useful book is *Herbs in Magic and Alchemy* C.L. Zalewski which gives astrological qualities and magical herb uses. My copy is from 1999 and is falling apart it is so well used. Another book with good basic information and lovely colorful pictures of herbs is *Herbs of the Northern Shaman* by Steve Andrews. Packed with information and general descriptions of selected herbs, it also includes magical properties, folklore, astrological ruling correspondences, and associated deities.

You can also find good and accurate information online but read widely to get an average of meanings. Record the information you find in a notebook or file for future reference.

Getting to know your herbs as a basic ingredient is desirable. Connecting with them equally so. You can take your time with this. How long you take to learn is entirely up to you and there is no time limit. In fact, it is doubtful you will ever stop learning. For more on planetary correspondences see the section on "Magical Days of the Week."

N.B. You can overdose on herbal medications, or they might be contraindicated with prescribed medication. Herbal does not necessarily mean safe. Do not ingest unless you are familiar with them and their contraindications or have visited a qualified herbalist.

Putting a Spell Together

When assembling your spell, you do not just choose several items and chuck them into a pot together. Think of it as cooking or baking, you would not choose random ingredients and mix them together, you would be a little more thoughtful and see what blends well, tastes good, and will be a good edible finished product. Magic is more of a precise art too. Choose each item you wish to use in the spell, carefully. Focus on what it will bring to the spell. Quality is better than quantity. Better to use a few items, which you have spent some time meditating on, than many items that you have chosen quickly (even if you know their properties). If you do not have the time, then ensure your intent is clear and focused during spell casting.

What happens if you feel you have not worked enough on a spell? Let us say you put together a favorite cake recipe that you know works well, all goes nicely, you put it in the oven then become distracted and burn it. You of course either abandon the cake making for now or begin again. The same applies to magic, if you become distracted, refocus, begin again, or abandon it until you have more time and fewer distractions.

Spells and charms come in many forms, so use whatever suits you. This all might seem complicated if you are a novice. However, with practice you build your background knowledge and what seems complicated now you will take in your stride later. If you are still building your competency in skills for sourcing ingredients, start with simple kitchen herbs. Learn the qualities of six to ten basic herbs.

Building up Ingredient Supplies

Many witches love to look within nature for ingredients for spells. Items sourced from nature have natural power. You also connect more with them. For instance, you go for a walk and spot something. You are attracted to it, pick it up and put it in your pocket. Alternatively, you go out with the express purpose of finding items but may come home with nothing or several things. In other words, you collect those items that you are attracted to and in choosing them are already building a connection with them.

It is handy to keep a little stock of ingredients collected from nature or taken from the kitchen or garden. For a spell, one ingredient can be swapped for another if you do not have it. For instance, for prosperity or money luck Rosemary, Bay, Mint, or Jasmine can be used in place of Basil.

Other items to collect that can be found in nature include feathers, pebbles, twigs (especially sacred woods, which can also be used as writing tools by scorching the end and using as charcoal), seashells, smooth broken glass, bark, leaves, flowers, herbs, and petals.

You can use items you find around the house or purchase especially. These would include a variety of candles (making your own would be ideal), ribbons (use old packaging, or gift ribbon), resins and incenses (you can make your own incense with herbs), crystals (if you use them and again is another item to purchase), and essential oils. More about these ingredients and their uses further below.

Herbs and Correspondences

Homegrown herbs or those picked from out in nature and dried are the best. Bought herbs are also acceptable if you do not have the space, garden, or even climate to grow them.

Below is a short list of herbs and other items from the kitchen, garden, and nature you might use in spell work. I have included ruling planets. This is by no means exhaustive and might not correspond exactly with what other witches and magical practitioners might use in spells, but I have found effective.

N.B. Not all the herbs and spices mentioned below are edible. Some are poisonous (i.e., Ragwort, Mistletoe, and Yew among others). Do not ingest before checking first and handle with care. Be cautious in incense use or if burning. Cross reference.

A Basic Herb Supply from Kitchen and Garden

Basil – Mars: Protection, luck, money, prosperity, purification, fidelity, love.

Bay – Sun: Protection, money, success, psychic work, strength.

Black Pepper – Mars: Protection, banishing.

Borage – Jupiter: Money and business, courage, joy.

Catnip – Venus: Protection, psychic work, courage.

Chamomile – Sun: Healing, psychic work, calming, luck.

Cinnamon – Sun: Psychic work, creativity, prosperity, money and business.

Clove – Sun: Venus, Jupiter: Psychic work, protection, money, general use.

Daffodil – Sun: Love, fertility, luck, repels negativity.

Dill – Mercury: Repels negativity, general luck.

Fennel – Mercury: Strength, courage, clairvoyance, protection, focus.

Flaxseed – Mars: Psychic power, protection, money.

Jasmine – Mercury, Venus: Luck, psychic work, hedge riding, visions, love.

Juniper – Sun, Mars: Protection, purification, revitalizing.

Lavender – Mercury: Happiness, love, psychic work, protection, purification.

Licorice – Mercury: Love, fidelity, binding.

Marigold – Sun: Harmony, prophetic dreaming, protection, divination.

Marjoram – Mercury: Balance, sleep, memory, love.

Mint – Venus, Mercury, Jupiter: Psychic work, uplifting, protection, prosperity.

Nutmeg – Moon: Psychic work, divination, memory, money, business.

Parsley – Mercury: Incense, flying ointment, protection, purification, raising of the spirits, love, luck.

Poppy Seed – Moon: Incense, fertility, hedge riding, protection, psychic work.

Rose petals – Red (**Jupiter** – Love, passion), White (**Moon** – Purification, truth), Pink (**Venus** – Love, friendship), Yellow (**Sun** – Luck, success).

Rosemary – Sun, Moon: Psychic work, love, protection, purification, uplifting, fidelity, mind clarity, luck.

Sage – Jupiter: Purification, protection, psychic work, memory, uplifting, healing, hedge riding.

Sunflower – Sun: Money, business, good luck, fertility, loyalty.

Thyme – Venus: Psychic work, concentration, purification, protection, balance.

Exploring the Hedgerows, Woods, and Meadows
The hedgerow is the perfect place to find ingredients for charms. You may not have hedgerows in the country where you live. A hedgerow is a hedge, sometimes a long one, of shrubs and trees, such as whitethorn (hawthorn), blackthorn, and elder. Hedgerows usually mark the border of fields and farmland. If they are on a busy road then you need to be careful if there are no pavements.

If you do not have hedgerows, then explore the grass verges, woods, and meadows instead.

Along the hedgerow and in woods and meadows you will find all manner of seasonal herbs, wildflowers, fruits, and blossom.

A Basic Herb Supply from Nature

Angelica – Sun: Incense, protection against evil, protection against spirits.

Celandine – Sun: Protection, happiness.

Clover – Mercury: Psychic work, protection, fertility, luck.

Coltsfoot – Venus (flower in March then leaf in May): Visions, peace, love.

Cowslip – Venus: Protection against spirits, beauty.

Dandelion – Jupiter: Psychic work, dreams, spirit contact.

Dog Rose (Usually pink or white): White (Moon – Purity, truth), Pink (Venus – Love, friendship.

Forget-me-not – Moon: Keeping a lover close.

Ivy – Saturn: Binding Spells.

Gorse/Furze – Mercury: Protection, divination, money, hope, strength.

Honeysuckle – Moon: Mind clarity, prosperity, love bonds.

Hyssop – Jupiter: Cleansing, purification.

Meadowsweet – Venus: Happiness, love.

Mistletoe – Sun: Protection, depression, fertility, healing, luck, love, inner strength.

Mugwort – Venus: Psychic work, protection, hedge riding (flying ointment), strength.

Nettle – Mars: Banishing, binding, protection.

Ragwort – Venus: Protection, hedge riding.

St. John's Wort – Sun: (most powerful at midsummer), protective, prophetic dreaming, money, and business.

Tansy – Venus: Love, longevity.

Valerian – Mercury: Love, protection, psychic work, money and business, graveyard dust.

Vervain – Venus: Love, peace, protection, purification, inspiration, good luck, psychic work.

Violet/Viola (Heartsease) – Venus: Love, rebirth, calming, protection.

Wild Thyme – Venus: Psychic work, concentration, purification, protection, balance.

Yarrow – Venus: Psychic work, protection, love, courage, divination.

Preparation of Herbs

In writing this section I do appreciate that not everyone is able to grow their own herbs. As I suggested above when you are able to grow them, they have more of *you* in them than bought ones. Even if you have not grown them from seed, you nurture them, and this has some impact on your connection to that herb. If you are growing your herb for magical purposes alone, every time you go to your herb and water it, or take a cutting, concentrate on why you are growing it. Try to at least grow some of your herbs. Pots on windowsills work well for some herbs such as basil.

The same applies for when you are out in the woods or countryside, hedgerows, riverbanks, or even road grass verges. If the herbs are specifically for spell work, you will already be thinking of this as you gather them. Try to avoid dog walking areas and busy roads to avoid pollution. Where I used to live, mugwort grew plentiful near the river. I would go to gather this especially and would think about the properties of the herb, concentrating on it and collecting it with good spirit, not forgetting to give thanks to the plant and to nature. Try not to gather herbs when you are stressed or in a rush. Setting aside time to do it, hanging, drying them out and putting into jars, all becomes part of the ritual and help your frame of mind and connections to the items you use.

But what about when you buy herbs? You can do this with the same spirit. There will certainly be more distractions, but with your newly heightened awareness – if you read the section on "Connection" and practiced the exercises – this task will be more meaningful. You can also buy pot plants from the supermarket or garden center, or buy packets of fresh herbs, which you can then dry yourself as more thought would go into it and therefore help with connection. Alternatively, you can premix your bought herbs for use as incense or for rolling candles in. For example, you could make a mix for protection or good luck. Refresh the mix if you do not use quickly.

Growing and Harvesting

Growing your own herbs can be fairly simple, such as planting in a window box indoors on a sunny window ledge or on a table to having dedicated tubs or space in your garden. Not being much of a gardener, for my own past herb gardens, I have just planted and left it all to providence, surprisingly with success. However, you can delve deeper into it and study books on growing herbs and vegetables and companion planting to help keep away pests. Occasionally, for some reason or another, an herb will fail to grow well or be attacked by aphids. I have found some staples easier to grow: Bay, Sage, Mint, Borage, and Thyme for instance. Rosemary does quite well in a pot.

Many pagans plant or harvest by moon phases, and it is certainly something to consider if you want to get the best out of your magical ingredients. Personally, I have harvested using moon phases but not used them to sow or plant. Many books have been written on this subject and you can buy almanacs and calendars to guide you. However, opinions differ, and information is varied, so be aware of this when looking for information and cross reference. Intuition will play a part.

Drying Herbs

Rose petals can be spread out on absorbent paper. Leave for a few days and put into jars. Natural drying is best. Avoid microwave and oven drying as it can cause the petals to develop an unpleasant odor.

Gather herbs and flowers on a dry day. If using for magic only and the herbs are free from pollution, no need to wash.

However, if intending to consume them too, rinse, and dry out on paper. Herbs and flowers can be tied in small bunches and hung from stems in a dark, dry place. Leave for a week to ten days to dry out.

To store, once they are dried, strip stems of leaves or flower heads if required, or break up into smaller parts and put into recycled glass jars such as jam pots, clip-top, or mason jars. If you have the space, you can keep herbs and flowers in bunches and hang in an appropriate place (though they can make a mess as they become drier and lose leaves). Alternatively, store longer stems of herbs or flowers in a larger jar and take a stem out as you wish (again after time they might fall apart). Using stems of herbs and flowers adds another pleasurable element to your magic. You are at once reminded of when you collected them and the magical intent you had in mind.

The Magic of Trees

To say trees are magical is an understatement. Apart from many of the many medicines that originate from them, trees reduce flood risk, improve air quality, absorb carbon dioxide, and release oxygen. For centuries, trees have been sacred to many cultures. More and more people are coming to realize the importance of them. To the modern witch, pagan, druid, and many others, trees are sacred.

In magic, trees have many uses. You can use the bark, leaf, twigs, branches, blossom, resin, and fruit to make amulets, spells, wands, writing materials, burning on the hearth or on outdoor fires, and for divination.

Identification

If you do not know the identity of many trees, buy a good book and use a camera or your phone to take pictures. Secondhand bookshops and charity/thrift shops are great places to buy reasonably priced books about trees. Ask for one for a gift. I inherited my own books from my mother and stepfather. There are many online websites dedicated to tree identification and to read about the mythology attached. If you suspect a tree is a certain species but want to be sure, then type it into a Google search and click on "images" and you should get more photographs for identification to compare with your own. You can also find plant identification apps free online.

Perhaps start with one or two species of tree. Take photos with you on your phone or print them off. You might have a small tree identification book that you can take with you. Or, if you can draw, sketch pictures. Alternatively, go on a nature walk with someone more knowledgeable. They will point out the features of a particular tree to make it more easily recognizable. A hawthorn for instance has thorns. It has blossom in spring and dark red berries in the autumn. When mature, leaves are small, dark green on top and have a light green underside. The blossom has five white petals (often tinged with pink) and yellow centers. The scent is liked by some people and found unpleasant by others. You can certainly smell hawthorn blossom when you are walking by. Make a point of looking for the chosen tree or trees each time you go out, so they become familiar to you.

When there are other species of tree close to the one you have chosen to collect from, this can make identifying leaves, twigs, and branches found on the ground more difficult. You only have to walk in the woods to see beech leaves mixed with oak and say hazel for instance. If you visit a grove of the same tree species, or a lone tree, then you will have more success. You can also compare branches, blossom, and leaves to what is still on the tree. Identification is much easier if the tree is in leaf or blossom. As time goes on you will be able to recognize even the tree bark more easily. Learning to identify leaves and bark will also help when you forage. It takes time, but you can build up basic skills.

You can apply the same principal with wildflower identification. Start with a handful of species or go on a nature walk with someone more knowledgeable. Herbs and flowers will change throughout the seasons, so be aware of this before you forage. It is no use looking for coltsfoot flowers in late summer. Again, take a book with you or take photos for later identification or sketch pictures. Another idea and one I have used when looking up a particular species, is by typing into an internet search something like "April yellow wildflowers UK (or Ireland)" and then searching through the images that appear until I find one that compares with my photo.

Harvesting

The basic guidance is to carefully harvest items from around the tree if possible and thank it. This is the usual advice for a reason, because taking branches and bark from the tree itself can hurt or destroy it. However, collecting fruit and blossom should be fine. A slight tug can dislodge a leaf that is ready to shed and the same with berries and blossom. Bark can be taken from larger fallen branches. You can generally find twigs, branches, leaves, fruit, and blossom around the tree. Sometimes these drop off the tree while you are looking for items – a gift to you. There are books that describe how to cut branches safely from a tree for use as wands, but it is up to you as an individual if you decide to do it that way and why.

Connecting with Trees

Overlooking the stage of making a connection with an item found in nature and the essential power within it, is a missed opportunity. When you use bark, branches, leaves, twigs, and blossom from a tree within your magical workings you connect with the tree's energy.

To draw on that energy, when you are collecting anything that has fallen from a particular tree then stay with it for a while. Touch the tree, hug it, converse with it. Note the location and return to it if you are able. You can maintain the relationship by periodically reconnecting with the items you have stored for future magical use or revisiting the original tree or woodland (this might be difficult if you keep items for a while as with time you lose track of where you found them, or they jumble with other items). For more about connecting with natural ingredients, please see the section "Connection."

Tree Meanings

Alder – Venus: Fire and Water, otherworld portal, purity, protection, divination.

Apple – Venus: Love, desire, temptation, immortality, calculated risk, plenty, wholeness, love.

Ash – Sun: Otherworld portal with Hawthorn and Oak. Ash is thought to be Yggdrasil, the world tree, but opinions differ. Its magical uses are justice, hedge riding, protection, prophetic dreaming, prosperity, spiritual growth, wisdom. Traditional wood of besom handles, and as the yule log. Yule/Winter Solstice.

Beech – Saturn: Communication, wisdom, inspiration, learning, fae wishes. Write or carve spells on wood.

Birch – Venus: Protection, protection of children, fertility, new beginnings, birth. Write spells on wood and bark. Besom brush. Imbolc/Imbolg. New Moon.

Blackthorn – Saturn/Mars: Protection, purification, grounding.

Cedar – Jupiter: Psychic work, money and business, longevity, prosperity, luck.

Elder – Saturn: Protection, shapeshifting, faery communication. Midsummer.

Elm – Saturn: (Elm has been ravaged by Dutch Elm Disease for decades. You still might find an odd one in the hedgerow). Death, rebirth, transition, protection, stability, empathy.

Fir – Moon: Enlightenment, perception, regeneration, protection, intuition. Dark Moon.

Hawthorn – Mars: Otherworld portal with Ash and Oak, faery communication, fertility, creativity, health, prosperity, purification, intuition, marriage. Beltane/Bealtaine.

Hazel – Mercury: Knowledge, wisdom, divination, inspiration, prosperity, marriage, protection.

Holly – Saturn: Life, vitality, protection, death and rebirth, banishing, fertility, healing, good luck. Yule.

Horse Chestnut – Venus: Health, luck, harmony, intuition, love attraction.

Oak – Jupiter: Otherworld portal with Hawthorn and Ash, strength, stability, courage, fertility, longevity, protection, success.

Rowan – Sun: Protection, divination, psychic work, strength, success, healing, perseverance.

Spindle – Sun: Industry, wealth, knowledge, weaving, blessing, fruitfulness, crafts, triple goddess, divination. Imbolc/Imbolg, Lammas/Lughnasadh. (Beware poisonous berries.)

Walnut – Sun: Knowledge, second sight.

Willow – Moon: Love, healing, renewal, fertility, peace, protection, communication with spirit world, astral travel, divination. Besom brush ties.

Yew – Saturn: Rebirth, transformation, regeneration, change, longevity, wisdom, psychic work, connecting with ancestors, visions, protection, divination. (All parts of the tree are poisonous. Take care around children.) Another tree that has sometimes been thought to be the Yggdrasil the world tree.

Magical Uses for Wood

Twigs

- Gather twigs from the same tree in bunches and label as it is easy to mix up woods. Use single twigs in magical herb bunches as part of a spell to keep on your altar as protection or for other magical purposes.
- Twigs also make good divining tools. Write Ogham symbols on them or other divination forms. Alternatively, label each twig and use them as they are as a divining method. Close eyes and draw out a twig. Use the properties of that wood to advise or guide you.
- Scorch the end of a twig suitable for burning and extinguish the flame. You now have a charcoal-like end to use as a pen to write messages, chants, and wishes for spells. Employ the properties of the wood in the messages purpose. Scorch the twig again when it no longer writes.

Bark

- Larger pieces of bark can be placed on your altar as a magical aid or around the house as a general boost – oak for strength, birch for new beginnings, ash for prosperity and so forth.

- The inside of larger pieces of bark can be written on, depending on the surface.
- Use shredded bark in magical herb pouches.

Branches
- Make wands from branches you can use in your magical practice to direct energy. You can have several types of wand (but ensure you know which is which).
- Slice wood into discs (these can be polished if wished) to make a rune set. Burn or paint symbols into the wood. You can make other forms of divination with twigs or draw on magical symbols for spell work.
- Great for stout staffs for walking, ceremony, or magical purposes. Use without decoration, alternatively, burn or carve symbols into it, make a handle, or varnish or polish. There are craftspeople who will do this for you.
- Use magical woods for lighting ceremonial fires. Use seasoned wood and ensure it is suitable for burning.

Blossom, Fruit, and Leaves
- Use in magical herb pouches.
- Use in incense mixes.

A Spell: Mistletoe and Apple Wood

Below is an example of how just two tree-related items can be used effectively within spell work, using the folklore behind them.

Mistletoe

When I moved into my current home, I was delighted to find a large ball of mistletoe in an old apple tree. Mistletoe grows prolifically in my area in different types of trees.

In *Complete Herbal,* Culpeper says of mistletoe ("misselto") that it is under the dominion of the Sun, but even though it "rarely" grows on oak, when it does it takes on the nature of Jupiter. From these two planets, I would say together they promote positivity, success, and good fortune, strength, wisdom, provide protection, represent the self, and have life-giving properties. You should also decide what they signify to you.

Culpeper also says he does not know why mistletoe takes on that nature of the oak (strength), above the other trees it grows on. However, he adds that mistletoe which grows on pear trees and apple trees, also "participates in something of his nature, because he rules the tree it grows upon" (but he adds it has more virtues when growing on an oak).

As mentioned above, in my own garden mistletoe grows on an apple tree. When I use it in magic, I then take this into account. I incorporate the qualities of both the mistletoe and apple tree together and in the spell example I hope will demonstrate how different items from nature can work together to assist in magical charms. I have taken the mythology mentioned below from my book *Walking the Faery Pathway*.

Culpeper says Clusius (a Flemish botanist), maintains that mistletoe when gathered should not touch the ground and that it protects against witchcraft.

Pliny (a Roman historian) also states that the Druids cut mistletoe with a golden sickle and confirms it was caught in a cloak so as not to touch the ground. As well as for medical uses, the Druids are said to have used mistletoe as protection against negative influences.

Additionally, there are other ancient mentions of mistletoe and in Norse mythology, the arrow that killed Baldur was carved from mistletoe. In the story, "all things" (these are plants, humans, and animals) were asked to swear an oath to protect Baldur from harm. However, the mistletoe was deigned too small and young to bother about, so the goddess Frigg failed to ask for an oath from it and it killed Baldur. (*Norse Myths, Gods of the Vikings*, Kevin Crossley-Holland, Penguin Books 1993 edition.)

This all shows that mistletoe is far from insignificant. Here we have an ancient myth pointing out the power of mistletoe and, significantly, how not to underestimate its power. Accordingly, putting aside the minimal uses (bearing in mind it is a poisonous plant so be cautious with it around children and pets), you can use mistletoe for protection. As a sun herb you can use it against depression (also healing, luck, and love).

Culpeper wrote:

The Vital spirit hath its residence in the heart, and is dispersed from it by the Arteries; and is governed by the influence of the Sun. And it is to the body, as the Sun is to the Creation; as the heart is in the Microcosm, so is the Sun in the Megacosm; and as the sun gives life, light, and motion the Creation, so doth the heart to the body.

The sun gives life to creation or the earth, and our hearts give life to us. We can use this plant in the following spell for self, general inner strength, and for fertility.

Mistletoe has male qualities and is of the Sun and Jupiter (especially if growing on an oak) and the Norse equivalent is Thor (Thursday). Suggested days for casting the spell are Sundays or Thursdays for success, joy, and strength.

The Apple Tree

The apple tree is a magical tree connected to the Otherworld and appears more frequently in folklore than, perhaps, any other tree, often taking an important part. Glastonbury's Avalon is called 'The Isle of Apples'. Linked to Avalon is the faery, Morgan Le Fey or Morgana. King Arthur was taken to the Isle of Avalon by the three faery queens when he was mortally wounded. The apple tree is linked with the Otherworld and journeying and is useful to the hedge witch. *Herbs in Magic and Alchemy* (C.L. Zaleweski) has apple listed among other properties as being used for love charms, enticing, temptation, indulgence, and aid in entering the underworld.

The apple itself is very much connected with the Celtic festival Samhain and many customs accompany the fruit for this day. Samhain is a time of year when the veil between the Otherworld and world of mortals is thin.

The apple is the fruit of the Otherworld. One was given to Thomas the Rhymer by the Queen of Elfland, and this gave him the gift of prophecy and a tongue that never lied. The apple features in fairy tales as with Snow White. The wicked queen tricks Snow White with the poisoned but beautifully delicious and innocent looking apple. The apple again, of course, features in the story of Adam and Eve, and reflections of this story can be found in the mythology of many other cultures.

A Celtic myth is also associated with the apple. In this tale, a strange faery maiden appears to *Connla*, the son of *Conn* of the hundred fights (or battles) and only he can see her. She tells him she comes from a fairy mound and is in love with him and wishes to take him back with her. Hearing this, Conn the king wanting to prevent it, asks for help from his Druid counsel who makes a charm. The charm causes the fairy maiden to disappear, but before doing so she throws Connla a magic apple. For a whole month, the apple is all Connla can eat or wishes to eat as he so longs for the maiden. At last, she returns, and they sail away together and are never seen again.

As you can see, the apple appears to be used as an enchanted weapon of seduction. It entices people with its delicious beauty (as in the faery tale Snow White) and is used as a symbol of sexual lust (the eating of the forbidden fruit), or the luring away of a man by a beautiful woman who promises much but for this he must give up his previous and normal life.

Finally, an apple can be used in divination. Old customs reveal that if you peel an apple in one piece and throw the peel over your shoulder onto the floor, whatever letter is formed by the peel is the initial of your true love's first name. Another form of divination is to stand in front of a mirror at Samhain and slowly slice an apple and eat it. Your true love's image should appear in the glass. However, if a skull appears, true love is dead to you. Also, with the apple tree's magical properties the wood is perfect for wands.

The apple tree brings wholeness and abundance. During this time of wholeness, it is easy to be seduced by outside influences, by beauty, and the promise of a better life. This is sometimes linked with passionate love. Passionate love can blind the eyes and stop you from seeing the world around you. Often where the apple is concerned, there is a choice to be made and that choice may mean a forfeit or giving up of something. This forfeit perhaps involves something stable (but mundane), which needs to be sacrificed for something that is more of a gamble or calculated risk (but is exciting). This does not mean the choice is wrong, however, it should be well thought out. Listen to any warnings that come from deep within you which you are likely to be ignoring.

The maiden seduces you with her beautiful and delicious but enchanted apple. She brings excitement and passion into your life, yet you still have a choice, and she rewards you with her gift of prophecy enabling you to make a better choice.

An apple tree and its fruit represent desire, temptation, immortality, calculated risk, plenty, wholeness, and love. Here we concentrate on the calculated risk, love of the job, wholeness, and plenty.

Apple is female and a tree of Venus. Friday is the day of Venus (or Norse Freyja/Frigg). Fridays can be added to Sunday and Thursday as a possible day to cast the spell. It will depend on the nature of the spell and the reason for casting it.

Bringing the Properties of Mistletoe and Apple together

For this simple spell I use mistletoe alone with its apple properties, or mistletoe with its apple properties and apple from the same tree. Autumn would be the best time for both the apple and the mistletoe berry. Alternatively, use leaves, twigs, blossom, depending on the time of year and what is growing.

The mistletoe rules over the apple tree it grows upon. It also takes on the magical properties of that tree. Mistletoe is protective and provides inner strength. The apple is seductive but also concerns taking risks, choice, love, healing, and intuition. The mistletoe will enhance the positive energies.

The protective qualities of both mistletoe and apple can be used in hedge riding to help you travel easily to realms and provide protection during the journey (place on lap or in your hedge-witch version of the medicine bag, the hagge bag).

Here we use it for more general purposes, success in a job interview. My imaginary tale begins with a man who is comfortable in his current job but has been head-hunted for a job with more money. The position he currently holds is boring but stable. He is familiar with the job practices and has had years of experience, so finds it easy. However, there is little room for growth, and he feels he is withering away. The pay is also lower than the wage he feels he deserves after his years of loyalty.

The job offered is challenging and managerial – so has more responsibility attached – offers more autonomy, a good wage, and is more diverse and exciting.

"Be careful what you wish for" is something he is concerned about. Will he enjoy the job if he gets it? Will it provide long-term security?

Therefore, incorporated into the intent of the spell, is that he wishes to be successful in his application, but only if the job is the right one for him. Again, be clear on the intent.

I could add the following elements to my spell, (you can keep it simpler.)

—My apple-tree grown **mistletoe** has **male and female** qualities. My **apple** female.

—Day of spell **Thursday/Thor/Jupiter**, and **Friday** for **Freya/Venus** (add **Wednesday** to include both the communication properties of **Mercury/Woden or Odin** and the magical number **three** (cast over three days).

—Norse Runes (my preferred divination practice). Any combination of the following. **Fehu** (this is Frey rather than Freya but is a good fertility rune), **Sowilo** (Sun, happiness, prosperity), **Ansuz** (Odin and communication), and **Algiz** (protection, wisdom, caution).

Casting the spell

- For a basic spell, the witch may well want to add more elements to the two main items such as a candle (perhaps gold or yellow for success and blue for communication), dressed in essential oil (frankincense for protection) and crushed herbs (rosemary for instance for luck). Construct the spell on your workspace or altar. Plain colored candles can also be used, dress in essential oil (frankincense and rosemary again) and roll in appropriate crushed herbs. Tie yellow and blue ribbons around the candle holder you use. Place the mistletoe and apple around the candle holder along with the other ingredients you have chosen.

- Suggested herbs to incorporate into the spell herb mix are a selection of black pepper, sunflower, parsley, clover, valerian, honeysuckle, thyme, basil, bay, borage, cinnamon, birch, and fir.

- Alternatively, for another type of spell, the practitioner can carry the mistletoe and apple (twig or leaf) in a magical pouch along with other ingredients if wished.

- Another method is to cast the spell by going out to the tree and placing your hands on it, tuning into the magical properties of both the mistletoe and apple (mistletoe could be high in the tree and impossible to reach without risk). Chant if wished. This can be repeated over more days.

- The fruit of the apple tree can also be incorporated into the spell. This can be eaten by you or the subject after perhaps carving letters into it beforehand.
- Perhaps compose a chant. When you concentrate on the spell and intent for several minutes on the day or each of the days (three times on each of the days, totaling a magical three by three or nine times), recite your chant.
- Alternatively, you can write your wishes on paper using burnt apple wood and burn the paper in the candle flame. Or carve words into your candle.

Before casting the spell take time to consider how you will go about it. Add elements as you see fit. More importantly, think clearly about the intent and what you want to achieve. As I say above there is no point in wishing for any job if any job will not do (anymore than in a love spell wishing for one particular person when that person could turn out to be the wrong choice for you or your subject). Be precise in what you, or they, want.

Other Magical Ingredients Found in Nature

Acorns (Properties of the Oak). Use in charm pouches and witch bottles, sprinkle on your altar and around your spell, carry on your person.

Bark (Properties of the tree from which it comes). Use in charm pouches and witch bottles, sprinkle on your altar and around your spell.

Berries (Properties of the tree from which they come). Use in charm pouches and witch bottles, sprinkle around spells and on your altar.

Feathers (Air: journeying, spirit messaging). Gather in bunches or lay on your altar. Alternatively wear the feather. Add to charm pouches and witch bottles.

Fir Cones (Properties of the fir tree). Use in charm pouches, lay on altar, or carry.

General Fruit of the Tree (Properties of the tree from which they come). For use in all types of charm pouches, witch bottles, and incenses (if suitable).

Hag Stones Use in spells to ward off illness, protection, and good luck. Hang from appropriate color threads. Couple with other items to increase power. In divination and prophecy use hag stones to look through.

Leaves and needles (Properties of the tree from which they come). Use in charm pouches and witch bottles, sprinkle on altar or around spells, crushed in herb mixes, incenses (if suitable for burning).

Metals (Correspondences below).

Nuts (Properties of the tree from which they come). Use in charm pouches and witch bottles, eat (if suitable), sprinkle on altar and around spells, carry on person.

Stones (All-purpose depending on the practitioner). Use generally for divination, healing, magical pouches, medicine bags, or carry on your person. Stones can be used in the same way crystals are for healing. Make a circle from your stones and place your spell or spell candle in the center.

Rose Hips Use in incense, charm pouches and witch bottles, herb mixes, make magical teas. (Love, protection, peace, healing, psychic work, luck, abundance, friendship love.)

Shells (Water, ocean, moon. Shape can add to meaning: a spiral means energy and power generation, journey from past to present, continuing journey). Add to charm pouches and witch bottles or lay on altar and around spells.

Snail Shell (Spiral: Energy and power generation, journey from past to present, continuing journey). Add to charm pouches and witch bottles or lay on altar.

Twigs (Properties of the tree from which they come). Use in bunches, witch bottles, divination, or lay on your altar.

Resins for Incense

Resins can be bought from spiritual shops and online.

Frankincense – Sun: Is the hardened resin from the Boswellia sacra tree. Use for psychic work, justice, cleansing, protection, consecration, meditation.

Myrrh – Sun: Comes from the tree genus Commiphora. Use for peace, enhancing magic, reviving, purification, protection. Also use in combination with Frankincense.

N.B. Tables and correspondences in this book may differ from system to system and practitioner to practitioner. I have included the ones I personally use and built up over the years, and you can alter as suited to your own research and what feels right.

Metals

Below are metals that you are more likely to work with.

Silver – Moon
Silver promotes intuition, spiritual energy, feminine energy, emotions, peace, and is purifying. Use silver for appropriate spells cast in conjunction with the Moon's phases.

Iron – Mars
Iron is protective against negative magic and curses, including faery magic. It is good for grounding, victory, strength, action, courage, and protection. The saying "bull in a china shop" comes to mind with Mars and Iron. If you have a tendency to battle, rein it in and keep it under control and you will achieve better results. Use iron in conjunction with the rune Uruz (Aurochs) for a quieter strength.

Tin – Jupiter
Tin has energy. It is for the adventurer. Use for spells involving travel, calculated risks, good luck, energy, strength, education, prosperity, success, ambition, and drive.

Copper – Venus
Copper is good for wand making as it is a good conductor of energy. Use in spells for healing, love, sexual energy, protection, warmth, money, love, and friendship. I have a hammered copper hare head. There are two magical elements. The hare symbolizing fertility and spring, and new ventures, and the copper and its magical properties. I use it to invite good energy for any type of new beginnings and fertility in new ventures, whether that is for a new or renewed relationship, a new business, love matters, general fertility, and healing. I ensure this is on my altar or table

when creating and casting the spells.

Gold – Sun

Gold is of the Sun and has the Sun's properties. Health, wealth, growth, happiness, and love. Use in spells connected with love, health, money spells, prosperity, success, and growth.

Both **Lead (Saturn)** and **Mercury (Mercury)** are unlikely to be used in everyday magic as they are toxic.

Runes

As I mention them several times in this book, and as you can easily make them with natural materials such as wood and stone, I thought it useful to give basic rune symbol meanings here. Runes (whichever futhark you prefer) are perfect for use in magic. My book *The Spiritual Runes* gives a history of runes, their meanings, ritual, magic, how to make a set and more. When using in magic it is advisable to learn more about them first.

You can carve symbols or draw on pebbles or etch in wood. I personally have several sets.

Search for suitable pebbles in rivers, beaches, or on the land. Stones often lend themselves to the rune symbol in shape, though you might want them all uniform. Collect them gradually and you will soon have enough for a set. Always keep spare stones as runes occasionally go astray.

According to the first recording of a divinatory rune casting written by Tacitus in the first century CE, fruit-bearing trees were used to make runes (they were scattered onto a white cloth after looking skywards and evoking the gods). For wood choose a fallen branch that is a suitable width and cut across to make small discs. Burn symbols on each. You can buy a pyrography tool for this. Symbols can also be painted on or carved. The discs can be varnished or stained to protect the wood or left natural.

Any size stone or wood will do when using magic. For divination you might want to use pebbles or wood that are a more manageable size for casting.

You can hold the rune when casting the spell to help you with intent. Alternatively, include in magical sachets, place around the main spell, carve into candles, or write on paper.

The rune meanings below are for the Elder Futhark. There are three "Aett's" with eight runes to each: Frey's Aett, Hagal's Aett, Tyr's Aett.

Runes and Keywords

ᚠ	Wealth (earned or won), possessions, good fortune, prosperity, sharing, luck, fertility
ᚢ	Strength (inner and outer but controlled), stamina, energy, fortitude, tenacity, independence, passion, luck, creativity, courage, good health, happiness
ᚦ	Protective, forces of nature, tribulation, adversity, survival of difficulties, self-assertion
ᚨ	Communication, wisdom, life-breath, inner voice, teaching, inspiration, persuasion, contentment
ᚱ	Journey, excitement, pleasure, adventure, transportation, change, movement, new experiences
ᚲ	Creative ventures, illumination, heightened sexual passion

X	Gift, happiness, praise, support, honor, nourishment
ᛈ	Joy, happiness, harmony, success, community, better health, prosperity
H	Crisis, limitations, restriction, disorder, change
ᚼ	Need, constraint, difficulties, help, survival, change
I	Ice, stagnation, freeze out, thaw, spellbound, spring
ᛋ	Harvest, bounty, prosperity, success, achievement, patience
ᛄ	Immortality, renewal, rebirth, protection, transition, reliability, steadfastness, quiet strength

ᚲ	Gamble, community, comradeship, solidarity, enjoyment, pleasure, risk, chance, creativity, luck, boldness
ᛉ	Caution, protection, advice, wisdom, talisman
ᛋ	Sun, light, optimism, direction, life-force, success, happiness, confidence, rebirth, new beginnings, encouraging, warming, nourishing, banishing, guide
ᛏ	Warrior, guide, justice, victory, strength, protection, wise counsel, reliability, honor, wisdom, self-sacrifice, courage, light in the darkness
ᛒ	Birch, spring, fertility, purification, new beginnings, luck, success
ᛗ	Partnerships, progress, movement, mobility, bonding, journey, vehicle, success
ᛗ	Man, Self, comradeship, community, compassion, talents, skills, inner progress

ᛚ	Emotions, flexibility, journey, energies, forward movement
◇	Fertile time, spring, seed, new growth, new phase or start, new relationship or romance
ᛗ	Hope, merriment, new start, change, transition, light, optimism, success, revelation, enlightenment
ᛟ	Estate, inheritance, possessions, family, country, community, peace, prosperity, security, harmony, grounding, safeguarding

How to Use Runes in a Spell

Imagine you wish to create your spell using only four items: **herb mix** (perhaps for rolling the candle in, or incense), **candles**, **essential oil**, and **runes**. If instead of just looking up what herb you should use for which spell and adding it in, you learn more about that herb individually, you become more aware of and more select in which ones to use.

In addition to learning what magical qualities each **herb** brings to the mix, forge a connection with them, perhaps starting by growing them yourself and then by spending time working with them. If you then make an incense or candle-rub mix, that mix will carry that much more magical weight.

The same principle applies to choosing **candle** colors. Rather than just looking up the meaning or which color to use, bring into the mix what that color means to you personally. Use your instincts. (More on Candle Magic in the next section.)

Again, with **essential oils**, learn about the qualities. If you roll the candle in essential oil and crushed herbs you add all those extra qualities to it. (And the crushed herbs mixture will also have had thought put into them while choosing them and again if you grew them yourself for magical purposes.) All this not only helps create the spell but also helps with intent and concentration.

Above I started with four items I would use for the spell example – **herbs, essential oil, candles,** and **runes.** With the last item, **runes,** you do need to study them. Once you learn the basic runes, how to make connections with them, and become more practiced, you can begin to learn about rune magic and bind runes. Doing your research to give you an in-depth knowledge of how they work together, will help you confidently incorporate them into your spells. Place rune stones around your candle holder. Another magical element to add to your spell is to carve rune symbols into your candle before rolling in the herbs and essential oil. Doing this becomes part of the ritual. Alternatively, draw runes onto paper in the form of simple messages and burn in the candle flame.

Putting a spell together with only four ingredients might seem simple at first glance, however, as you can see above there is a wealth of knowledge behind each one. If you already use runes, it will be easier. If you are new to herbs, then choosing a handful to start with to make your mix will simplify the process.

You can follow complete recipes (there is nothing wrong in this), but I do find it more powerful and satisfying to build and put together my own. Keep notes about spells for future use. You can modify recipes to suit.

Candle and Color Magic

There is not the space for a comprehensive delve into candle magic, owing to this book being a short guide, however, I do feel it is worth a mention as so many practitioners use candles in spell work at least some of the time.

When we read about the meanings of color in magic, we most often find them logical. They fit in with our own idea of what they represent – Red is fiery, Blue is calming or cool, Orange has vitality, White is pure, Purple is spiritual and so forth. Therefore you, as the magical practitioner, can also bring in the qualities that they represent to you personally.

Candle color magic can be used for sympathetic magic in that often a petitioner candle representing the person who is requesting magical help is used in addition to the candles of intention rather like a poppet. I use this personally, depending on the spell.

Basic Color Correspondences

Red – Fire: Vitality, Vigor, Sexual Potency, Passion, Energy, Courage, Willpower.

Pink: Love, Romance, Friendship, Devotion, Affection, Honor, Health.

Yellow – Air and Sun: Happiness, Optimism, Abundance, Intellect, Creativity, Careers, Success, Good Fortune, Prosperity, Attraction.

Orange: Confidence, Ambition, Energy, Optimism, Success, Drive, Action, Communication, Strength, Joy, Encouragement.

Green: Matters of the Heart, Healing, Fertility, Money, Prosperity, Good Luck, Growth.

Blue – Water: Balance, Communication, Empathy, Peace, Harmony, Balance, Healing, Honesty, Loyalty, Spiritual Matters, Inspiration, Wisdom.

Purple: Psychic Awareness, Clairvoyance, Spirituality, Spiritual Energy, Dreams, Inner Happiness, Astral Projection.

Brown – Earth: Homestead, Practical Matters, Harvest, Endurance, Grounding.

Black: Protection, Acceptance, Change, Absorption of Negative Forces, Banishing, Binding. Defense.

White: Purity, Peace, Truth, Cleansing, Innocence, Light.

Grey: Uncertainty, Confusion, Tiredness.

Silver – Moon: Secret Dreams, Intuition, Meditation, Divination.

Gold – Sun: Happiness, Attraction, Success, Money, Abundance, Good Fortune.

Adding Color to Plain Candles

If you run out of a particular candle color and only have a plain white or cream-colored candle add color to it. If gifts or flowers come with colored ribbon, keep the short lengths for magical purposes.

Embroidery threads and wool will also work. Tie around the candleholder rather than the candle itself to avoid fire risk.

If you have a garden, in the spring and summer, flower heads or petals can be used. When a rose is past its best, the centers are often still good. Remove and dry by placing on paper towel for a few days. Store in bags or jars. As the rose color also has magical properties these serve a double purpose. Other flowers such as lavender, cowslip, dandelion, and valerian also have dual purposes – color and properties. Use berries in the autumn or winter. You can do the same with bought flowers. Save the centers and dry. Place these around the candle. Or tie to candle holder.

Peel such as from an orange or lemon can also add color.

Colored pebbles and crystals are useful especially if they have magical properties. You can also put aside a few colored glass beads used to decorate bottoms of vases if you have any, and smooth broken glass collected on beaches.

Save colored glass bottles to use as candle holders.

Another idea if your spell is over three days is to cover it with the appropriate colored cloth in between use (ensuring the candle really is extinguished first).

Candle Dressing

I thought I would add here a little about candle dressing. I have in this book mentioned candle colors and that you can roll your candles in essential oil and herbs. To do this make your herb mix and crush it using a mortar and pestle. Rub an appropriate essential oil or a carrying oil on to the candle. Often it is recommended to do this from the center outward, though opinions may vary. Then roll the candle in the crushed herbs. All the time you do this, concentrate on the purpose of the spell.

Spell Example: Bringing People Together

In creating a spell to bring people together, choose one candle to represent each. The color of these candles will depend on the colors you associate each person with or might depend on the reasons they grew apart. Say one person has anger issues (red) and the other is confused and indecisive (grey). The two candles could be placed at each end of the altar or a shelf (I have done this on a mantlepiece and window ledge). Place a third candle in the center, say of a harmonizing calmer color such as blue or pink or even both. The blue will act as a communication tool and for peace, and the pink for gentle love. Each day, over perhaps nine days, light the candles and bring towards the center candles while concentrating on the goal.

You can use color alone for the spell or with other items of that color such as crystals, stones, flowers and so forth. Other elements can also be added to the above spell, such as crushed herbs and essential oils used as a candle dressing. Runes can be carved into the candles perhaps Gebo (Gift) for connections, or Ehwaz (Horse) for partnerships and bonding.

Spell Example: Money

Below I have used a yellow or gold candle to represent money. Many witches use green as it is the color of money in the US (but this is not so in many countries). Gold (or yellow) to represent gold, good luck, and success is my own preference.

- Gold or yellow candle (or neutral and if required decorate with color using ribbon, wool, or cord).
- Brass candle holder (gold, silver, yellow, or plain are fine).
- Citrine (if you use crystals). Place close to candle holder.
- Flaxseed (to represent money though coins can also be used).
- Base oil for candle dressing (suggestions: sunflower, flaxseed/linseed, rosemary, chamomile).
- The runes FEHU (Cattle) for wealth and prosperity (earned wealth), and URUZ (Aurochs) for inner and outer strength. Place staves next to the candle, carve into the candle, or draw them on paper and burn in the candle flame (have a flameproof dish handy).

Herbs (any mix of the following)
Basil (money and luck)
Bay (money)
Borage (money)
Cinnamon (money, prosperity)
Clove (money)
Clover (luck)
Rosemary (luck)
St. John's Wort (money)
Valerian (money)
Vervain (luck)

A yellow or gold cloth (a scarf will do)

N.B. All the above ingredients are optional. You do not have to include everything. Your intent is more important. Please adapt the spell as necessary. Add chants or other elements as you wish.

Method

Mix herbs and crush in pestle and mortar or with rolling pin. Carve the rune symbols into the candle (if this is your preference).

Rub oil onto the candle from the outer end inwards.

Roll in the crushed herbs.

Place candle in the holder.

Sprinkle flaxseed (or coins) all around candle and holder to represent money.

Every day for three days leading up to the full moon burn the candles for a few inches and concentrate on your wishes and desires. Visualize you or your subject being successful in your quest (receiving a work contract for instance).

Burn the rune symbols on the last day if you have not carved them and they are drawn on paper.

When not in use, cover the candle in a yellow or gold cloth (ensure it is extinguished).

Magic and The Elements

Below are the four basic elements to incorporate into your magic.

Element of Water

Water connects to the west. Water is essential to all life – to human life, animal life, plant life. We source power from water. Water is cleansing, literally and to wash away negativity. Water can be both calming and destructive. It flows fast and furious as do our emotions and is associated with the emotions.

Emotions are fluid. Think of the saying "lost at sea." Often, we are lost at sea when we are experiencing a flood of confusing or unhappy emotions. However, emotions can also be overwhelmingly happy – floating or swimming in a "sea" of them.

In tarot, the suit of cups is associated with water and inner experiences, emotions, and feelings.

The rune Laguz (Lake) is associated with water and the emotions.

Water is to fold thought endless when they sale forth
on an unstable ship. The great waves of the sea terrify,
And the seahorse heeds not the bridle.
—The Old English Rune Poem
(from *The Spiritual Runes*, Harmonia Saille)

Of course, water is changeable, so you can be sailing in or into a storm on the sea but can also sail along on a gentle breeze. Sometimes you might become becalmed and not move at all, become stuck – "Isa" the "ice" rune represents this.

A blue candle represents water, but also calmness, spirituality, harmony, healing, fidelity, loyalty, and wisdom. You might also use more than one candle color, depending on what you want to achieve.

Water Spells

Water spells are ideal for spells centered around healing and the emotions. Floating candles are ideal for working with both. They can still be dressed or carved into like any other candle. As well as your candle, float other things in the water such as rose petals and herbs.

Bath spells also are very effective for healing and the emotions. For this, make up a bag of herbs. You will need to choose ones that are non-poisonous and will not irritate the skin. Muslin or cheese cloth is a suitable fabric to use. Tie the bag tightly at the top or sew it shut as you do not want to end up covered in herb flakes and having to shower them off.

I have used lavender, rose, thyme, sage, parsley, chamomile, and rosemary, among others for bath spells – mainly herbs you can also make tea out of or add to cooking, but so check for contraindications. If you prefer, use essential oils instead.

If you do not have a bathtub, you can still use the bag in the shower. Wet the bag and squeeze the herbs, letting it drip over you. Rinse off. This is especially beneficial if you want to rid yourself of negative energy. Water is a great purify and cleanser. Bath spells can help wash away the remnants of a broken relationship and encourage a new start.

Spell Example – Bath Banishing

Ingredients:
Chamomile
Lavender
White rose
Marigold
Thyme
Parsley
Muslin or cheese cloth
Frankincense incense sticks

White candles

N.B. Do not use any herb that you think you might have an allergy to.

Sew a bag into a square using the muslin, leaving the top open. Alternatively, cut a square of the fabric.

Choose a mixture of herbs from the above list and place in the bag or in the middle of the square. Sew the top up or gather the ends and tie tightly.

Run your bath and leave the bag to soak for a few minutes.

Light your candles and incense (ensure adequate ventilation). When you are ready, lie in your bath and splash yourself all over with the cleansing bath water. Imagine the negativities leaving your body and picture your new start be it leaving an old demoralizing job or ridding yourself of leftover feelings from an old relationship. When you are finished, stay in the bath, pull out the plug and watch the water drain away, taking all the negativity with it.

Element of Fire

Fire connects to the south. Fire is creativity, inspiration, passion, warmth, sex, fertility, energy, power, and is both destructive (but allowing for new growth) and purifying. As the sun it is the giver of life.

In tarot the suit of wands is associated with fire. It represents life, courage, energy, inspiration, warmth, light, creativity, willpower.

The rune Kenaz (the torch) is associated with fire.

The torch is to the living, known by its flame.
Shining bright, it burns most often,
Where the nobles rest, inside the hall.
—The Old English Rune Poem
(from *The Spiritual Runes,* Harmonia Saille)

This stanza tells us that the torch burns more brightly inside the hall where it is controlled. People sit together in its light presumably mulling over events, talking. It implies learning and wisdom. It lights the room so we can see each other and our way forward. It is creative, positive, and illuminating.

Fire Spells

For spell work, we light candles and the flame encourages the magical vibrations to go out into the ether. Red candles represent fire and are used for all sorts of energy spell work. If used to fire up creative ventures, then orange is a good accompanying candle color. Orange also provides strength, vitality, creativity, encouragement, stimulation, sexual energy, and joy.

If you have a fireplace or a firepit outside, burn suitable seasoned magical wood (logs or twigs), using the magical meanings from the earlier section on trees. Concentrate on your intent while watching the wood burn.

Festival Fires

Below are a few suggestions for wood burning:

Imbolc/Imbolg
Willow (love, healing, renewal, fertility)
Birch (fertility, new beginnings, birth)

Spring Equinox
Birch (fertility, new beginnings, birth)
Oak (fertility, longevity, protection, success)

Beltane/Bealtaine
Oak (fertility, longevity, protection, success)
Hawthorn (fertility, creativity, health, prosperity, purification)

Summer Solstice
Hazel (inspiration, prosperity, marriage)
Elder (protection, shapeshifting, faery communication)
Beech (communication, wisdom, learning, fae wishes)

Lammas/Lughnasadh
Spindle (industry, wealth, knowledge, blessing, fruitfulness)
Ash (prosperity, spiritual growth, wisdom)

Autumn Equinox
Spindle (industry, wealth, knowledge, blessing, fruitfulness)
Ash (prosperity, spiritual growth, wisdom)
Apple (plenty)

Samhain
Hazel (knowledge, wisdom)
Elder (protection, shapeshifting, faery communication)
Beech (communication, wisdom, learning, fae wishes)
Apple (plenty)

Winter Solstice/Yule
Fir (enlightenment, perception, regeneration)
Ash (Yule log), (prosperity, spiritual growth, wisdom)
Holly (vitality, protection, death and rebirth, banishing, fertility, healing, good luck)

Element of Earth

Earth connects to the north. Earth is practical and physical.

In tarot the suit of pentacles is associated with earth. Earth is the practical side of life, dealing with material things, basic needs, and earned income.

There are several runes I would associate with earth, including Ingwaz (God Ing of fertility), and Jera (Harvest or Season). To work with earth, I have chosen Othala (Homestead or Own Land).

The estate is dear to every man.
If he can take pleasure in what he has,
More often will prosper.
—The Old English Rune Poem
(from *The Spiritual Runes,* Harmonia Saille)

If man take care of home matters, the everyday things in life, he will prosper.

Earth Spells
Magical work often includes spells surrounding practical matters: family life, home life, accommodation, work, income. For practical matters, brown or green candles are most used. Brown is used for grounding, earthly matters, matters of the home. In conjunction green is often used for spells for finances, but also for health and healing. You can bury spells and witch bottles in the earth.

Spell Example – Prosperity for the Self or Home

Ingredients
(Choose five or use own replacements)
Basil
Lavender
Clove
Mint
Parsley
Yellow rose petals
White rose petals
Clover
Rosehips

Lavender essential oil (optional)

(Choose one or use own replacements)
Horse Chestnut: Bark chippings, leaf, twig, or fruit (Conker)
Hazel: Bark chippings, leaf, twig, or nut
Holly: Bark chippings, leaf, twig, or berry
Brown, black, yellow (or gold candles)

Gather the ingredients in a bag or cloth and place on your altar. Take some and grind together using a mortar and pestle. Dress your candles in lavender essential oil or carrier oil and roll in the mix.
Light your candles.
Concentrate on the black candle absorbing negativity and expelling through the flame.
Concentrate on the brown candle to keep you grounded, and for help dealing with all matters for the home and home life.
Concentrate on the yellow (or gold) candle to bring good luck, prosperity, and protection, coming to yourself or your home. When the candles have burnt down. Take the rest of the ingredients and dig a hole outside if possible close to your home. Tip the ingredients in (do not bury the cloth if you are suspicious that it is not biodegradable) and cover over while concentrating on your goals. Give thanks.

Element of Air

Air connects to the east. It correlates with spring and beginnings. Intelligence, thoughts, mind, balanced thinking. Air is also creative.

Air Magic

In tarot, the suit of swords is associated with air.

For me personally, Ansuz (The Mouth of Odin or God Rune) equates with air.

The mouth is the source of all speech.

It is the support of wisdom, and the wise man's counsel,

And to the noble warrior it is inspiration and happiness.
—The Old English Rune Poem
(from *The Spiritual Runes,* Harmonia Saille)

The verse relates to the rune Ansuz and to speech, wisdom, inspiration, and happiness. Ansuz, like Air, is inner voice, intellect, communication, inspiration, wisdom, life force, vision, knowledge, and contentment. I have found that Ansuz also connects to creative efforts particularly writing.

Include the rune "Ansuz" in your Air spells concerning any of the above.

This rune, Berkano, although the element earth, relates to the spell below and new beginnings.

The Birch is fruitless, still it bears
twigs without fertile seed, its shining branches
high on its crown loaded with leaves, reach to the sky.
—The Old English Rune Poem
(from *The Spiritual Runes,* Harmonia Saille)

For color magic, yellow is often used for matters and spells pertaining to "air". Yellow is spring, beginnings, the intellect, success, happiness. White is occasionally used in its place. White is purity, peace, and innocence.

Air spells are effective cast out of doors where you can feel the breeze upon your face.

Spell Example – Beginning Again

Sometimes we all need to begin again. This could be after a job loss, after financial loss, the end of a relationship (or the death of a partner), moving to a new area, even the need to begin a new creative project.

This is a basic spell. To it appropriate herbs can be added to fit the reason for the new beginning. As usual I have given you a choice of herbs and other items to choose from. I encourage you to find any replacement herbs (if you do not have those listed or cannot get them) and use your own growing skills to add other ingredients as you wish.

Cast at dawn, facing east. If possible, do this on a spring festival (Imbolg, Spring Equinox, Bealtaine) then it will have that extra power boost. A New Moon is a good alternative.

Basic Ingredients
Birch bark, or green leaves (if they are out)
Yellow candle
Rosemary (for clarity of though)
Honeysuckle
The rune Berkano (drawn on paper)
Bag or cloth for charm sachet (please see how to make a charm sachet/magical pouch in the section following "Magical Bottles" below this section).

For job success after loss or after financial loss – add the rune Fehu (fire/earth: for practical matters and earned wealth) and Mannaz (air: for dealing with people effectively). Herbs: Basil (money); Borage (money/business, courage, and joy); Clove (money and business; Daffodil (luck); Fennel (focus and strength); Mint (prosperity). Tin (good luck, energy, calculated risk, success, drive, strength).

To begin again after a relationship end – Berkano (earth, important for new beginnings and fertility). Add Raidho (air, travel) to help you move out of your comfort zone and start a new adventure. Herbs: Chamomile (healing): Mistletoe (fertility, healing, luck, love, inner strength); Willow (healing, renewal, fertility); Yarrow (courage, protection). Copper (healing, protection, love and friendship, fertility).

New creative project or to break writer's block – add the rune Ansuz (air, communication, learning, writing). Herbs: Vervain (inspiration); Honeysuckle and Rosemary (important for mind clarity); Juniper (revitalizing); Hazel (inspiration); Spindle (industry and fruitfulness); Beech (inspiration, wisdom, learning).

To help you settle in your new home and area – add the rune Othala (earth and practical matters), and Sowilo (air and success). Herbs: Thyme (protection and balance); Mint (prosperity); Daffodil (luck and future success). Gold for health, wealth, growth, happiness, love.

Sowilo the sun (air) can be added to all of the above for future success and the "light at the end of the tunnel."

Preparation and Casting
Use a selection of ingredients or use a good replacement.
Crush herbs.
Using a carrier oil and suitable essential oil. Dress the candle with oil, roll in the herbs, and place in holder.
Open up your cloth or sachet.
Light the candle and concentrate on your aims, hopes, and dreams. Tip the herbs, tree bark, leaves, metals, and runes into the sachet and close. If you have drawn runes, include them in the sachet or burn in the candle flame, keeping focus.
After you have finished, carry the sachet with you generally and for interviews or job searches, visiting financial advisors, and house viewings, or visits to new premises, jobs, or areas.

You can read more about the elements in my *Pagan Portal* book, *Hedge Witchcraft*.

Magical Bottles

The Witch's Bottle

A spell used in past times and of which there is remaining evidence is the witch's bottle, and this is still used by many a modern witch. Traditionally used against witchcraft or bewitching, we still use it for protection, or perhaps to defend against or deflect negative energies.

The traditional witch's bottle would contain such things as pins and nails, thorns, nail clippings and hair, human or animal urine (again from the bewitched human or animal as a counter measure), and cloth hearts (sometimes pierced with pins). The bottle was concealed somewhere, perhaps buried, or heated until it exploded. The offending witch, in turn, would suffer a slow and painful death unless the bottle was uncorked. In the case of the heating of the bottle, the effects were instant once the bottle burst. The witch would die, and the victim freed. If the bottle became uncorked, it was the witch who was freed.[1]

A few years ago, on the UK TV show *The Antiques Roadshow* (BBC 2019), a presenter tasted the contents of a 150-year-old bottle (yuck), which he thought was a bottle of port wine. I was shouting at the TV, "No, don't drink it!" as I recognized what it was. Later, it was analyzed and was found to contain brass pins, a human hair and, yes, some alcohol, but the other ingredient was urine. One other item it contained was an ostracod (a crustacean). I have tried to discover the magical significance of an ostracod, but, needless to say, this could have had a personal connection to the witch or whoever made the bottle up. It may even have got into the bottle accidentally. From research ostracods have several pairs of legs, like a crab, and are tiny, sometimes being called a "seed shrimp." The "expert" would not have necessarily known what the bottle was, but the clue to it being a witch's bottle was that it was unearthed at the threshold of a house.

Of course, the contents of the witches' bottles mentioned above do not have to be adapted, as all the ingredients can be found. I have made a variety of protective bottles, but not as a victim of a bewitchment. I have it on great authority that it is still used by some witches, and I certainly would not rule it out, depending on the purpose. Another way urine would still be used as an ingredient in the modern witch's bottle is as a defensive measure, though there may well be more ways that witches use it.

One idea of the witch's bottle in modern times is perhaps that the bewitcher would themselves suffer the fate, which they had wished upon the victim. This can be seen as "reap what you sow" or reflecting the magic back to the perpetrator.

Another type of witch's bottle, which has been found in the Netherlands, was a type of protective bottle or jug. The bottles were discovered in Culemborg, which is coincidently a town where I lived for several years. Protective bottles such as this were usually in the form of simple stoneware jugs. These were found buried under houses built after a great fire in 1422, as a protective measure. Jugs of this kind often contained oats or eggshells.

Owing to jugs unearthed containing old coins, it is thought many of the jugs found in the Netherlands were probably filled with substances which were tipped out by the person who dug it up to look for money, and seeing none, would just keep the empty jug. Some of the jugs were found buried upside down more often under the threshold of the house. The purpose was perhaps to trap evil spirits (as was sometimes the case with the witch's bottle in the UK). The jug was also believed to be buried upside down to save soil getting into the bottle and leaving no space for the spirit. The oats and eggshells in the jug were thought to act as bait or as an offering, and any coins perhaps acted as a talisman. However, with no other mention of the jugs or evidence to back it up, this is conjecture. One suggested purpose of the jug was to be as a home for the guardian spirit of the house, but this is less likely.[3]

While living in Culemborg, I buried my own bottle on the boundary of my home as a protective measure. In this case, I packed it with protective herbs. I then filled the bottle with wine; this in addition to drowning the negative energy soaked in through the porous cork, was a libation to the spirits and Earth if the bottle was broken. If the bottle is broken however, the charm also loses its power.

Below are three ways to make a witch's bottle. One is based on the traditional British witch's bottle (adapted for protection), and the other based on the Dutch protection witch's jug, with the third for trapping negative entities.

Witch's Protection Bottle

A glass bottle (Must be glass so it is biodegradable. This can be any type of bottle; a beer bottle is suitable if it can be stopped with a cork. I have some that have a witch's head on, which is quite nice. A smaller bottle can be used and is easier to bury, again if it has a cork that fits).

A cork (or use a metal lid).

Blackthorn-thorns (Blackthorn is a good ingredient to use to protect your property as it creates boundaries. Be extra careful collecting the thorns as they can pierce the skin and cause the wound to go septic and it can be quite painful for a while. If you cannot find thorns, use pins or nails or a mix of all three)

Human hair (of the person needing protection)

Human urine (of the person needing protection)

Human nail clippings (of the person needing protection)

The **Witch's Bottle for Protection** should be finished off by pouring urine over the contents in the bottle. How you collect the urine is up to you, though for the ladies it might be a bit hit and miss if you try to pee straight into the narrow top, in this case better to use a jug first. Alternatively, use wine. Seal the bottle with the cork, and further with red wax if preferred. Bury or conceal in the place you have chosen.

Witch's Protection Jug

Small pottery jug (that can be stopped with a cork, otherwise use a glass bottle)
A cork (real cork, not plastic)
Blackthorn-thorns (or pins)
Rosemary (I like this as it has needles. Must be fresh rosemary not dried unless you dried it yourself, so the needles are longer)
Protective herbs (anything you wish to add such as sage or black pepper)
Red wine (to drown the negative energy, and as a libation should the bottle break)
Small shells (optional: the shell's purpose is to protect)
Sea salt (optional: salt is naturally protective)

After preparing the **Witch's Protection Jug** by layering the various ingredients in the jug or bottle, fill with the red wine. Seal the bottle with the cork, and further with red wax if preferred.

Spirit Trap Jug

Small pottery jug with lid (otherwise a glass jar or bottle)
A piece of natural material in an appropriate color (to use to cover the mouth of the jug, jar, or bottle)
A quantity of oats or crushed eggshell
A few coins (optional)

The **Spirit Trap Jug** should be part filled with the eggshells or oats (or perhaps a mixture), along with coins if included. Leave a space in the jug for the negative entity. Close with the lid and cover the end with the cloth and tie securely. Bury the jug upside down in your chosen place or lie on its side if concealing rather than burying.

Putting it All Together

In each case fill the bottle with dry ingredients and then follow the instructions below for the individual bottle or jug. Do this within a magical setting as you would for any spells. Concentrate on the purpose of the spell before and during the preparation. Have in mind a place to conceal or bury your bottle. Places often used were chimneys, beneath the threshold, under the floor, behind the walls and on the boundaries of the property concerned, depending on the purpose of casting the spell. After you have finished all the preparations below, take some time to empower your spell further by visualizing the protection it will bring or whatever the final use will be.

Scrying Bottle

I have fond memories of the village of Feakle in County Clare, Ireland, where a well-known witch of old, Biddy Early (1798–1874) lived for a time. She perhaps fully represents the female witch of old as we might imagine her to be. It was here that Biddy, who was said to have red hair, developed her reputation for her herbal remedies and healing. She was also said to talk to the fairies or be "away with the fairies." She had a "blue" bottle that contained dark liquid that she would consult when seeking a cure for the ailment. Effectively scrying the future. One story concerning this was that a farmer believed his herd of cattle cursed by the fairies. Biddy determined the problem using her bottle and told him that he had planted a whitethorn (hawthorn) on a fairy path and that he must remove it. Once removed his cattle were restored to health.

Biddy was married four times in all (though it could be between three and six) and widowed each time it seems. One of her husbands was only thirty when she was in her seventies, but she still outlived him as he died of alcoholism. People came to her for cures for the ailments and for charms. She was eventually accused of witchcraft and brought before a court in Ennis (the county town of Clare) in 1865, unusual for this time. But the witnesses against her backed down and she was released through lack of evidence. Biddy is now buried in Feakle graveyard. Her bottle was never seen again, said to have been taken back by the fairies. However, there is also a story that the local parish priest threw it into a lake. Stories about her continued into the 1950s by the people who knew her. Biddy Early was very much a true witch as we would use the term today (rather than someone who was accused of witchcraft who was entirely innocent of witchcraft practices).

The story above shows us two things: the first that divination was used in folk magic in past times and indeed there is history of that. The second thing is that divination is a useful skill to have when practicing magic.

For scrying you can use a number of items, a crystal ball, a scrying mirror bought or made, or a black bowl filled with water or dark liquid.

You can scry into many things, so the subject is worth further study. Biddy Early used a blue bottle filled with dark liquid. (As a suggestion a blue bottle filled with water and colored with black ink would work.) You will be scrying to shed further light on the problem for which you later intend to create a spell to solve. Find a quiet spot and by candlelight and ensure you have time as it can take time for symbols to form and for you to interpret them. The resulting divination hopefully will throw light on the type of spell you should go onto create.

Example of Symbols Seen

This example shows how divination can assist you in spell work. The symbols in this example that were seen when scrying are a bee and a beaver. Remember when divining symbols to use your intuition. Meanings can come quickly to mind.

Bees can symbolize a number of things, however, in this case both bees and beavers have something in common, they are hard workers. If we couple this with you having a shortage of money, the symbolism of hard work indicates the money should be earned by you. The spell you create might center around earned money and the ability to earn, luck in having that work come to you, and the physical and mental strength to complete the work. In many ways a standard money spell should suffice as a basis.

Below, the guide to animal symbolism to help you in scrying and hedge riding is necessarily short and this book is a short guide. Buy a good book (or two) on symbolism and use your intuition in addition.

A Quick Guide to Animal Symbolism

Ant: Perseverance, self-discipline, virtue, stamina, industry, group effort, orderliness. (Hard work brings results. Involve others to help.)

Antelope: Solar-lunar, grace, beauty, fertility, awakener. (For help in relationships.)

Badger: Lunar, fierce protector of home, supernatural power, mischief, cunning, stoutness of heart. (Overcoming obstacles and protector.)

Bat: Dual nature, swallower of the light, guardian of the night, good luck, longevity, peace, wisdom, health, wealth, happiness, rebirth, obscurity, darkness. (Nature of relationships. Meaning should be divined along with other symbols to give an overall picture.)

Bear: Lunar, power, strength, intuitive, mediator between man and god/s, maternal, fierce protector. (Nurturing and caring for others. Need to control anger.)

Bee: Industry, order, purity, soul, love, messenger, wisdom, community, harmonious living. (Help in working at relationships, employment.)

Beaver: Builder, gatherer, home, family, group achievement, industry. (Working at family relationships. Involve others to help.)

Blackbird: Enchantment. (Be careful whom you enchant.)

Boar: Solar, warrior, leadership, direction, strength, fearlessness, solitude. (For help when great strength is needed.)

Buffalo: Prayers granted, abundance, fortitude, curing powers. (Brings all good things. Quiet inner strength.)

Bull: Solar-lunar, male and female strength, divination. (For help when different types of strength are needed. Prophecy.)

Butterfly: Metamorphosis, transformer, rebirth, marital happiness, new beginnings, communication with higher worlds. (For help in new relationships, new beginnings, or in radical change.)

Cat: Lunar/solar familiar, stealth, desire, liberty, clairvoyance, prophetic, magic, change, rejection of restraint, immortality. (For independence of body, mind, and spirit. Divination.)

Cockerel: Solar, courage, guardian, supremacy, valor, fidelity, victory. (Warns of danger. Help winning battles.)

Cow: Lunar, nourishment, motherhood, plenty, procreation, nurturing, maternal, hope, life cycle, psychopomp. (Providing life's necessities. New home luck.)

Crane: Solar, discipline, messenger, longevity, communication, wisdom, good fortune, happiness, wisdom, intelligence, psychopomp. (For help in new ventures and decision making.)

Crow: Messenger, familiar, solitude, communication, fidelity, shapeshifter, omen of change. (Bodes well for relationships. Predicts change or need for change.)

Deer: Gentleness, gracefulness, messenger, sensitivity, purity of purpose, swift, nimble, wealth, psychopomp. (Helping you to do the right thing. Providing guidance in times of need.)

Dog: Solar, familiar, guidance, protection, loyalty, fidelity, faithfulness, guardian, friendship, partnerships, psychopomp, rebirth. (As a friend when in need of moral support.)

Dolphin: Solar, hasten slowly, virtue, savior, guide, intelligence, communication, protection, psychopomp. (Your personal guide, directing you in life.)

Eagle: Solar, divine spirit, power in battle, protection, clear vision, courage, victory, pride, strength, free spirit, spiritual instinct. (For inner strength and help in overcoming adversity. Seeing the bigger picture.)

Frog: Lunar, fertility, new life, transformation, bringer of rain. (For new beginnings, fertility, or change.)

Goat: Vitality, virility, lust, procreation, fertility, abundance, creative energy, vision, independence. (To revive or control the sexual side of relationships. Fertility. For help in creative or independent ventures.)

Goose: Solar, watchful, protector, inspiration, happiness, providence, conjugal fertility, seasonal change, divination, shapeshifting. (Seasonal change. Commonly used by the witch in shapeshifting. Home. Love and fertility in relationships.)

Hare: Lunar, familiar, rebirth, rejuvenation, fertility, intuition, transformation, craftiness, shapeshifting. (For help with fertility, new ventures, and new starts.)

Horse: Solar, stamina, mobility, strength, loyalty, travel, intellect, connection, wisdom, wealth, freedom, duality, prophecy, psychic, psychopomp. (Helping you on a journey – either spiritual or actual. Partnership.)

Hummingbird: Magical, optimism, sweetness, joy, resurrection, love. (Magically assisting in matters of the heart. Happiness and optimism.)

Lion: Solar, guardian, power, majesty, strength, courage, pride, nobility. (Watching over and defending you. To give you courage.)

Salmon: Knowledge, instinct, persistence, determination, wisdom, inspiration, rejuvenation. (Helping you in decision making and in gaining knowledge.)

Serpent: Solar and lunar, rebirth, regeneration, healing, intuition, knowledge, wisdom, destroyer, fertility. (For help in regeneration of self or ventures. Healing. Wisdom.)

Spider: Creative, spinner of destiny, divination, creating possibilities, prophetic, money luck. (For prosperity. Divination.)

Charm Sachets and Herb Bunches

To make simple sachets a light material works best – muslin/ cheesecloth, gauze, or any light natural material. You can also use material that corresponds to appropriate colors.

Take an oblong piece of material and fold it in half. Sew side seams. You can make a hem at the top and thread through ribbon or cord to close, otherwise add herb mixes and sew top seam to seal. Alternatively, cut a large circle from the material and draw together the edge with running stitches or hem it and thread through with cord to make a round pouch. You can glue or staple bags. Sachet bags are generally available online to buy if you so wish.

To make bunches. Pick and gather herbs together and tie at the bottom. Use fresh or hang to dry. If wishing to use as a smudge stick, when herb bunch has dried out, wrap cotton, or string around it from bottom to top (each round should be half to one inch apart).

If you use ribbon or string to tie bunches and sachets in the appropriate color correspondence, it will also help identify the purpose of each.

You can embroider letters, magical symbols, or runes on the outside of the bag. This will remind you of the sachet's purpose and add an extra magical boost.

Fill bags with dried herbs. Add other magical items such as shells and stones if you wish.

Sachet Recipes

Some of the below can also be made into bunches to lay on your altar or hang over doorways or windows. More herb meanings in the ingredient section.

Protection Sachet
Use a selection of the following herbs:

Bay
Black pepper
Catnip
Sage
St. John's Wort
Thyme
Woods: Alder, Oak, Birch, Elder, Rowan

Inspiration Sachet
Use a selection of the following herbs:
Cinnamon stick
Juniper
Parsley
Rosemary
Sage
Woods: Hazel, Fir

Prosperity and Success Sachet
Use a selection of the following herbs:
Borage
Basil
Bay
Cinnamon stick
Mint
Parsley
Woods: Ash, Fir, Hazel, Yew, Oak

Love and Happiness Sachet
Use a selection of the following herbs:
Basil
Clover
Jasmine
Lavender
Meadowsweet

Mint
Orange peel
Parsley
Rose (pink)
Rosemary
Viola
Woods: Apple, Horse chestnut

Psychic-Work Sachet
Use a selection of the following herbs:
Borage
Catnip
Clove
Mugwort
Parsley
Sage
Thyme
Woods: Ash, Cedar, Cypress, Walnut, Willow

Hagge Bags

Hagge bag is my own name for a hedge witch's medicine drawstring bag or bundle that helps you connect to your spiritual self. Hagge (Middle English) comes from the longer Old English word haegtesse and means "witch." There is evidence of medicine bags across cultures and history. Some shamans use them. In Norse mythology, *Erik's Saga,* said to have been written in the thirteenth century and of which two versions are preserved, *Hauksbók* and *Skalholtbók,* there is a mention of *Seidh* or *Seidr.* In this story, a priestess, a *Völva,* carries a belt with a skin pouch containing magical items. Seidh bears some similarities to shamanism. The *Völva* (or seer) was seated on a high cushion stuffed with hen feathers. A special song was sung to summon the spirits, enabling her to go into a trance to seek answers to questions for members of the community. I once took part in such a ceremony in Belgium and had a question answered that I did not even ask. A message was given to me instead. But it was the answer to something specific that had been playing heavily on my mind and the advice was invaluable.

A hagge bag does not have to be purely for hedge riding or shamanic journeying. You can, indeed, keep it on your lap during journeying, but also open or carry during rituals and spell casting, or when you need extra support or healing energy.

For your bag use a large piece of cloth, such as a handkerchief or headscarf and knot at the top. Alternatively use a drawstring bag that you have bought or made out of natural material.

Gradually add items to your bag that have come to be special to you magically, connecting to them first. This might include a stone, crystal or rune, small hag stone, a feather, piece of bone, shell, acorn, bark, herbs, or petals. Anything that is "good medicine" to you and that together build a powerful energy to heal and protect.

Keep the bag sacred to you.

Animal Familiars

Animal familiars are animals that assist you in your magical working and are not to be confused with animal guides or power animals. I have not always been assisted by familiars when practicing magic, though during my time as a witch we have always had animals in the home, generally cats and dogs. The two black cats we have now, old as they are, would not lend themselves to be good magical companions and the psychic link is missing though plenty of love is there. The last cat I had as a familiar, Parsley, was a tabby and a good magical companion and always accompanied me during magical work and rituals.

In past times, especially during the witch persecutions, familiars were said to be spirits masquerading as household animals. These familiar spirits could shape shift and were used as spies. The witch was often accused of feeding the familiar, though with blood instead of demanding or stealing breastmilk from other mothers or animals. Worse still, of turning milk into blood. Teats were said to be found near the witch's genitals or anus.[4] Terrible for any of the accused who had a wart or mole in those areas.

In modern Pagan times, Animal familiars are generally animals you already have in the home, a pet such as a cat, dog, reptile, rodent, or adopted bird (I knew someone who had a crow who would come to the windowsill).

Often you feel a connection to this animal from the start though you can develop a better bond with a suitable pet by spending more time with them. Look out for the following when deciding if your pet would be a good familiar.

- You have an instant connection to them, psychic or emotional.
- They found you rather than the other way around.

- They came into your life at the most unusual time.
- When you first met, you needed each other and had an overwhelming feeling the relationship was meant to be.
- They always want to join in with your magical workings such as casting spells, rituals, and divination.
- They are calm as you work.
- They appear to listen to and watch you (rather than just go to sleep).

Below is further information about the more popular choices for animal familiars:

Birds

Birds are dwellers in the world tree. Owing to the abilities of flight they are mediators and are the spiritual link between the heavens and earth, communicating between the two. Birds are the prophets and messengers. If you have a wild bird coming regularly to your windowsill especially during your magical workings, you are very lucky. Talk to it and make polite requests. Ask it to carry your messages out into the world and up into the heavens. Be open to receiving psychic messages too. Does a common thought connected to your spell work keep popping into your head? Take note.

Cat

Cats are both lunar and solar. They are psychic and like the rat have the powers to predict disaster. Cats appear prominently in mythology. For instance, Artemis took the form of a cat when fleeing from Typhon. The cat was sacred to the Egyptian god Set and the power of darkness and to the goddess Bastet. In Norse mythology two cats pull Freyja's chariot as she controls the night. In other cultures, cats occasionally have negative connotations.

As a familiar, cats represent stealth, desire, independence, and freedom. They have the powers of clairvoyance, sometimes foretelling the future, and have exceptional magical qualities. Often changeable in personality they will refuse to be confined. Make sure they are around during your magical workings or when divining. Take note of when they appear agitated and protective of you or if they withdraw and hide during your magical practice. Is their change in behavior trying to impart something?

Dog

Dogs work well as a protective familiar. They are Solar but can also be lunar. They protect the light. Associated with Artemis, the goddess of the moon and the hunt they can act as spiritual mediators. As guardians they can guide and protect. Dogs are both psychic and psychopomps. Their loyalty, fidelity, faithfulness, and friendship are unquestionable. A dog is a good familiar to have around to protect you during your magical workings and shamanic or hedge riding journeys.

Rat

In Hindu mythology a rat is the steed of Ganesha, the elephant-headed god of wisdom, prosperity, and success. They bring good luck. They are also said to foretell disaster, so take care if you suspect they are trying to tell you something with their changed behavior. In your magical practice rats are good to have around if your spell work is primarily around bringing luck and happiness. But take care if your rat wants to "leave the sinking ship." In other words, be cautious. Ensure your home is safe and do a check if necessary. Do not leave burning candles unattended.

Serpent/Snake

Solar and lunar, the serpent is mostly seen as masculine owing to its phallic shape. Regularly shedding its skin, it has the powers of healing, rebirth, and renewal. As a winged serpent they are mediators between gods and humans. When a snake appears in a shamanic journey or hedge riding, they often impart knowledge and wisdom. In Chinese mythology they relate to the Yin symbol (earth and water) and also to female energy and the moon, and is dark, passive, wet, and cold. In Norse mythology the snake is Jörmungandr, the Midgard sea serpent, that tightly surrounds the earth, biting its own tail. It is a symbol of the constant threat to disruption on earth, and after releasing its tail, is there at Ragnarök spilling its venom. The symbol Uroborus, the serpent also biting its own tail, represents eternity or infinity, and regeneration and recurrence. In alchemy, the Uroborus symbol represents change. Serpents are wise and remind us that we are all on the wheel of life and can fall off if we go too fast or lose our way, but we can climb back on but have to begin again, and although this brings change it also brings renewal. The serpent is the enchanter and will assist in magical workings around regeneration of self or in new ventures. They will add power and wisdom.

Your Magical Space

How the witch arranges his or her sacred or magical space is entirely up to the individual. This could be a small space in your bedroom or study. If you are lucky and have the space, then you might even have a room dedicated to your magical practices. It should be out of the way of the family and visitors.

The more workspace you have the more items you tend to have. In one house I lived in I was lucky to have a dedicated room with a lake view for my spiritual and magical practice. I had a large altar and chairs to use for hedge riding. Often several of us witches and pagans would meet up for group hedge riding. On my large altar I would have candles, candle holders, incense burners, bowls and dishes, mortar and pestle, pictures, hares, tools I found helpful (usually knives), wands and sacred woods, bark, stores of herbs, essential oils, pebbles, shells, feathers, and my divination tools (runes, tarot, scrying mirror, and crystal ball).

Now I have very little space and use the minimum of items and the rest has been stored away. It is a nuisance having to root through two boxes when I need something. So, just do what you can and have the space for. Herbs can be stored in kitchen cupboards or the bottom of closets. A drawer dedicated to magical items. A shelf or set of shelves in the garage or shed (if you have one) is also useful.

Do we need an altar?
It depends on your personal preference. An altar (or craft table if you prefer) needs to be big enough for putting together spells and keeping handy your scissors, knife, string, pins, or any other bits and pieces you might use in a spell. Say for instance you are putting together a bunch of herbs and wildflowers, if you have ever created a flower arrangement, or indeed just filled a vase

with flowers then you know this makes a little mess. Clean up once you have prepared your spell.

A chest of drawers can make a handy altar. You can keep your supplies in the drawers and use the top for your altar. This is great to keep tucked away your candles, charcoal, resins, ribbons, and anything else you might use. If it has a cupboard too, then you have somewhere to keep your herbs, divination tools and so forth.

Lack of Space

If you live with your parents, children, or share with friends, you could use a simple upturned cardboard box or any type of box for your table or altar and keep it in your bedroom. Cover this with a cloth or scarf. The good thing about this is it can be any size you wish, and you can customize it to the size of your space. After you finish with your magical workings, you can pack it all away inside the box.

Some people are so limited with space they use window ledges and have essential supplies only. A collapsible table is also useful. This can easily be transported to outdoor sites such as stone circles and woodland. You can use a kitchen worktop to create your spells. This is not always practical if it a busy area. However, a small occasional or coffee table might suffice.

Outdoor Space

There is something very special in casting spells outdoors. Try it if you get a chance. I have been lucky enough at times to have natural outside altars, which include an enormous limestone rock and a massive tree stump. Other times for outdoor workings, I have had nothing but a tiny stool. The ground can also be your altar and has the convenience of being anywhere you like.

If you leave items outside in all weathers, they do tend become dirty or rusty unless you cover them in inclement weather. Therefore, it is best just to leave only natural offerings outside and items such as lamps and take in anything you do not wish to spoil.

Magical Equipment

Do you need tools? Do they have to be consecrated? This again depends on your personal preference and practices. Tools (this does not include ingredients) may consist of a knife or scissors for cutting. If you wish to use a wand it can be as simple as a small branch of magical wood. You do not have to buy expensive metal or polished wood wands (there is nothing wrong in doing so if this is what you prefer). If you practice candle magic, then a candleholder or holders will be essential. The same with incense burning when a fireproof dish or cauldron in which to burn it will be handy (ensure the room is amply ventilated). But again, it is up to the individual.

If you wish to cleanse items, because you or others have previously used them for general purpose or others handled them, then pass them through a purifying smoke, such as frankincense, wash them in running water, or place under a cleansing waxing or full moon. I keep all items used for spell work for this purpose only, and do not use them generally.

Ritual

Ritual is part of spell casting. Within hedge magic the length of ritual is up to the individual as you construct your own pathway. The ritual for me is in everything I do to prepare for the spell: gathering and picking herbs, deciding what the other ingredients will go in the spell, finding a few quiet moments to build the spell, considering what it is I am trying to achieve, chanting, and spending time concentrating on my intent. You will soon find your own way of working, your own form of ritual that helps you get the best from spell work. Below are a few things to consider when doing this.

Protection

Psychic protection when creating spells is up to the individual. Some witches prefer to cast circles as part of the ritual or build protection around themselves such as a protective egg of light. Other witches find it unnecessary for simple magic, especially if they do not cast negative spells.

Ethics

In past times the witch would, most likely, curse as well as bless. In modern times we tend to have personal ethics and often only use positive magic (some witches do curse, and this is entirely up to the individual). The witch is not so much a black or white witch nor the magic itself, it is how you use it that makes it black or white or what puts it in a gray area. Some witches follow the threefold law or law of return in that everything you send out returns to you threefold. Others, me included, think that if a spell feels negative then it likely is, so avoid it. I do not follow the three-fold law exactly, but I do believe that what you send out reflects on you in some way. Negativity attracts negativity. Be as positive as you can during low times and make plans where you can. If you think negatively those vibes are going out there into the cosmos.

There is an old belief that bad luck comes in threes. If we look more closely, we may find that those things that recently happened to us actually happened to others and only affected us in a small way or made us sad. We look for the two other bad news events to get the three things over with. In fact, negative things happen to us all the time. And, if you examine your recent past closely, good things happened to you and others within that time. For instance, a friend becomes ill, your husband loses his job, and you think you have rheumatoid arthritis. Out of the three events only one of them directly involves you and is your own personal bad luck. The other two affect you in varying ways but are actually the bad luck of others. If you go to the doctors and have rheumatoid arthritis ruled out, your friend recovers with treatment, and your husband swiftly find a new job, you do not tot up these positive events as you do the bad ones. Yet the positive things are there all the time. When negative things happen to you view them as individual events and view the positive things as events alongside them to invite positive energy.

Going back to ethics, perhaps you feel you can cast a negative spell without feeling negative and many witches do. However, if you prefer to only use positive magic consider the following: in this scenario you wish to get your own back on the man or woman who ran off with your wife or boyfriend (please do count this as not being gender specific), or on the person who was promoted over you as he/she/them claimed your work was theirs. However, you cannot do a spell without anger and revenge vibrations seeping through. So how do you use positive spells only? You could do a spell for truth and justice. Or to help you get over the hurt and attract good luck into your life. Another way is to cast a spell to be recognized for your good work. With all these you are casting a positive spell to counteract the negative.

Counteract anything negative aimed at you or others, with cleansing, protection, strength, happiness, justice, luck, and so forth, or most likely a combination of some of those. For instance, if someone is indeed wishing you ill at work perhaps and scuttling your chances of promotion then use the combination of luck, strength, and protection. If someone is wishing your relationship to fail, then use the protection and happiness combination. And if your relationship has broken up, perhaps your partner has left you for someone else, then use the cleansing and strength combination (also use the protection if anything negative is aimed at you); then when you feel ready, use the happiness spell, and encourage new positive beginnings.

There are plenty of witches who will disagree with my own personal ethic and who do not believe in a law of return. Casting curses and using black or grey magic does not perturb them in any way. These witches have an entirely different mindset and are happy with their choices. Again, it is all down to what you personally believe. What I personally believe is that anger does not always last long. And you may do something to someone else that could end up affecting you. For instance, you cast a spell that your ex splits up with her new man and comes back to you. This happens. And then three years later you find out that she has been unfaithful to you during the whole period, and you just wasted three years of your life. That person deep down might not have wanted to come back but felt an irresistible pull.

Focus and Tuning in

First, practicing meditation is good for you. Just a few minutes three times a week is helpful, though every day is better. Meditation helps you focus even when you are not meditating. Meditation helps lessen anxiety and stress. It even helps your memory. With spell work it will help you keep focus on the task in hand.

Even though you might spend less time on a spell, perhaps

a half hour from preparation to casting it is important to be able to "tune in." Just as with meditation when you need to rid everyday clutter from you mind, the same is true of spell work. Additionally, you need to have a heightened level of awareness. Twilight is a good time to do this. It does not have to be actual twilight, a time of the "in between," where it is neither night nor day and magic abounds (though it is actually a good time to practice divination and magic), you can make a twilight-like atmosphere if you wish to help you with atmosphere. In the daytime draw curtains, try to cut out as much light as possible and use soft lamps and candlelight. In the evening, light candles. You might have an addition of moonlight filtering in, which will help. Anyone who can see auras or energy knows that this twilight-like light assists you in tuning in more to the aura or energy. This atmosphere is also a good time for spell work. Alternatively, working in sunlight is perfect for positive spells of happiness or success.

Heightened Awareness

Most of us lack awareness even in everyday tasks. We get up and go into auto mode. Without even realizing sometimes, we go about simple tasks without thinking what we are doing, such as brushing teeth, taking medication, or making coffee. Then later you think, "Did I take my medication already?" Our heads are everywhere but on the task. We sit on a bus or train and when we arrive at our destination cannot remember anything we saw on the way, even though we were looking out the window. We go for a walk in a park or in nature with the purpose of getting exercise and often fail to acknowledge the beauty surrounding us, coming home and not remembering part of it as our thoughts were elsewhere.

Learn to be aware. Take note of what you are doing when you do it. Keep concentrating on the task you are performing. Even the simple tasks. When out walking, look around you. What do you see, hear, and smell? Take note of even the smallest thing. The leaf blowing across the ground for instance.

Both meditation and improving your awareness helps you stop mind chatter and helps you focus.

Intent

Intent is the most important part of the spell. It is the reason you are casting the spell in the first place. The purpose. When you have good focus, you find when it comes to communicating your intent to a higher power and out into the universe you can concentrate better. The intent should be clear as I wrote earlier in the book, but I cannot emphasize this enough. An example, if we look back to a money spell, is that if you just asked for money in general then that money might come to you in the way of a loan, but it will have to be repaid perhaps with interest. If that is okay as you will have the opportunity to pay it back soon and you need money instantly, then all is well and good. If that is not the case and you lack money in general, you should instead ask for the wherewithal to earn that money, a job to enable you to do so for instance, then that money is yours to keep (though the tax man might want some).

Deciding intention before you begin preparations for the spell will help strengthen the power. Write it down if you need to. By the time the spell is completely prepared, and it comes to spending time on intent, you will have it clear in your mind.

You do need several minutes of quiet time while communicating your intent. Many witches also find it helpful to visualize the hoped-for result of a successful spell. (For example, receiving the certificate for the educational course passed.) If you find your mind is wandering, then speak your intention out loud. Be precise. Learning to focus will help prevent blocks from happening.

Timing

Part of a ritual might include a time you prefer to work your spell, with perhaps the time of day, evening, or Moon phase, coming into consideration if you decide this should be a part of your magical practice. You do not have to include any of these. You may wish to keep your spells and charms simple. Alternatively, you may want to include one or two elements.

Magical Days of the Week

Not everyone will agree on the colors or other elements included in this book. They will differ slightly from practitioner to practitioner.

The herbs mentioned below are ruled by the planet corresponding to the day of the week. They will also work with the "Spell Purpose" mentioned. You can also use other herbs that might fit in with the "Spell Purpose" regardless of ruling planet. This is entirely up to the witch who may well think that other herbs fit the purpose of the spell better.

All planets are given as Roman gods. I have also included lines from the old nursery rhyme "Monday's Child," as it is a reminder of what spells to cast on which day.

Monday
Planet: Moon (and its phases)
Color: Silver or white
Herbs of the Moon: Honeysuckle, Nutmeg, Poppy seed, Rose (white), Rosemary, Willow
Spell Purpose: Cleansing, purification, peace, emotions.
In the old Rhyme "Monday's child is fair of face" fits well here.
The moon is "fair" (beautiful) as are her qualities.

Tuesday
Planet: Mars (Norse god Tyr, Greek god Ares)
Color: Red

Herbs of Mars: Blackthorn, Flax seed, Gorse/Furze, Juniper, Nettle.

Spell Purpose: Battles, justice, victory, strength of will, courage, passion, protection.

"Tuesday's child is full of grace" may not on the surface fit well, however, in battles if you use inner strength and control it will gain you more positive results.

Wednesday

Planet: Mercury (Teutonic/Norse Woden/Odin, Greek god Hermes)

Color: Blue

Herbs of Mercury: Fennel, Hazel, Jasmine, Marjoram, Parsley.

Spell Purpose: Communication, wisdom, knowledge, messenger, writing.

"Wednesday's child is full of woe." Wednesday's child is more serious and intellectual than energetic but may also at times be in another realm.

Thursday

Planet: Jupiter (Norse God Thor, Greek god Zeus)

Color: Blue/Orange

Herbs of Jupiter: Borage, Cedar, Mistletoe, Oak, Sage.

Spell Purpose: Energy, strength, ambition, prosperity, success, leadership, education, travel.

Jupiter corresponds with the sign of the Zodiac Sagittarius. Sagittarius is adventurous and free spirited and "Thursday's child has far to go" fits perfectly here.

Friday

Planet: Venus (Norse goddess Frigg or Freyja, Greek goddess Aphrodite)

Color: Green/Pink

Herbs of Venus: Apple, Basil, Coltsfoot, Rose (pink), Tansy,

Vervain, Viola, Yarrow.

Spell Purpose: Healing, love, friendship, romance, money.

In the old rhyme "Friday's child is loving and giving" fits perfectly here with the love elements of this day.

Saturday

Planet: Saturn (Greek god Cronus)

Color: Black

Herbs of Saturn: Cypress, Elder, Holly, Ivy, St. John's Wort, Yew.

Spell Purpose: Banishing, absorbing negative energy, binding, exorcism, protection, endurance, diligence.

"Saturday's child works hard for a living" fits well here with endurance and diligence. Sometimes we cannot avoid hard work and working hard achieves results, exhausting as it is.

Sunday

Planet: Sun

Color: Yellow or gold

Herbs of the Sun: Bay, Celandine, Chamomile, Cinnamon, Clove, Daffodil, Juniper, Marigold, Mistletoe, Myrrh, Rose (yellow), Rosemary, Rowan, Sunflower.

Spell Purpose: Happiness, beauty, success, prosperity, good fortune.

"The child that is born on the Sabbath day is bonny and blithe, and good and gay" as you would expect reading the properties above.

Magical Times of Day

Before we even consider magical times of the day to work your charm, we first need to consider when you will find a quiet time to give yourself a few undisturbed minutes in which to work. Again, you cannot do this with the children or animals running around or likely to burst in on you, or if your partner or roommates are due in from work or college, or anytime you are likely to be disturbed. If you can arrange it so you can also work at a magical time of day, then obviously this would be perfect.

- **Dawn and Early Morning** (compare to the New and Waxing Moon) – New beginnings: Use the coming light of dawn for positive spell work, when a new start is needed, and for attraction, and purification.
- **Noon** (compare to the Full Moon) – This is when the sun is high in the sky, a positive time especially on a sunny day, for all positive magic: prosperity, creativeness, strength, and inviting luck and love.
- **Sunset** (compare this to the early Waning Moon) – For ridding yourself of negative habits, any sort of banishment, saying goodbye to an old love.
- **Midnight** (compare to the end of the Waning Moon as it slips into the Dark Moon) – Use your mental broom to sweep away the negative, the old, to make way for the new (the new day).

There is no hard and fast rule to this, and other magical practitioners might have their own idea of what time of day to cast a spell and for what reason.

Moon Phases

New Moon: New beginnings, new projects, putting plans into action, blessings, ideas, creativity, healing, prosperity.

Waxing Moon: Increase, growing of ideas, development, energy, attraction.

Full Moon: Protection, powerful magic, luck, strength, psychic power.

Waning Moon: Decrease, banishment, ridding of negative habits, ridding of bad health, endings, taking time out towards the dark moon to reflect on the coming light and what you have learnt from your negative experiences. During this time of stasis, plan for the future.

Length of Spell

One Day or less: This can be anything from a few minutes concentrating on a charm to hours of burning a candle right down until it uses up the entire wick.

Three Days: If burning a candle, then you would burn one third per day. Each time you light it, concentrate once more on the goal, and imagine your purpose achieved.

Nine Days: Taking several minutes to concentrate on your intent, burn a candle for a short while each day. You can separate a candle into sections by pushing pins horizontally into it as deep as the wick. When the flame reaches the pin, the pin pops or falls out. Blow the candle out and burn it to the next pin the following day. On the last day, burn the candle down until the entire wick is used and it goes out.

You can use a combination of time of day, moon, and spell length. Say you wanted to concentrate on or to encourage a new beginning, you might choose the time of the new moon, spread the spell over three days beginning at dawn each morning.

When spreading the spell out into three or nine days, cover with an appropriate color cloth when not in use (and ensuring the candles are extinguished). For positive spells cover with a yellow or gold cloth, for strength cover with a red or orange cloth, for protection cover with a black cloth, for purity a white cloth and so on.

Chants

Chants are useful and improve the spell, adding extra power. Chanting during spell casting is not a new idea. Again, referring to Reginald Scott's *Discoverie of Witchcraft* written c.1584 he mentions how saying words or verses not only adds efficacy of the spell, but the spell depends upon it. (Below I have modernized the text this time to make it easier to understand.)

To enchant, or (if you had rather have it so) to bewitch. In these enchantments, certain words, verses, or charm are secretly uttered, wherein there is thought to be miraculous efficacy. There is great variety hereof: but whether it be by charms, voices, images, characters, stones, plans, metals, herbs, etc., a special form of words must always be used, either divine, diabolical, insensible, or papistical [relating to the Roman Catholic Church so perhaps from a prayer book or the Bible], whereupon all the virtue of the work is supposed to depend.

Note the other ingredients here: images, characters, stones, plans, metals, herbs. After not being sure what was meant here with "plans," I did at first wonder if it was a misspelling of another word. After a search, the etymology was unclear for that time. However, the only other time "plan" is mentioned in this lengthy book it has the missing end letter "t" though it is in a similar context. Both "plant" and "planet" come up often in the book, but most likely, in this context, it is "plant."

Ritual Preparation

All the above phases of the moon, times of day, and length of charm, are part of the ritual. Finding a quiet time is also part of the ritual, as is planning your ingredients, what you will use in the spell. Choosing herbs, a ribbon or candle color, are all part of the ritual. All the time you are taking to plan the spell or charm, goes into the intent.

While we quietly work away at our magic our intent is powerful, our awareness is heightened, we are disciplined, and we are already tapping into the invisible cosmic forces, which by the time we have finished the spell work, we will nudge into a certain direction and hopefully bring events into manifestation.

You may think, "But this does seem as long and drawn out as casting a circle." But actually, when you get used to doing spell work, you gather ingredients, choose a time of the moon, or day, or how many minutes, hours, or days you intend to spread the spell over, in a relatively short space of time, rather than hours. Five minutes spent on a simple folk spell is too short, but two hours is rather long. As long as you feel you have worked on it enough, that you have put in enough power of thought, that you have done all you can do, then do not worry too much. It will soon come as second nature. It all comes with practice.

Magic in Hedge Riding and Visualizations

This section involves magic in hedge riding and journeying, but also how you can enhance your magic using simple visualizations if you are not a hedge rider. There are many similarities between journeying and hedge riding. A person who practices shamanism might well have followed a shamanic practitioner course, but then hedge witches might have too, to strengthen their knowledge of the realms they visit. Purposes might differ. A hedge rider might use journeying for magical purpose, while a shamanic practitioner for healing or soul retrieval. As a hedge rider I have also used ridings for healing and personal development as might a journeyer.

A hedge witch, if we look at the where the term originated, flies to the other worlds for the purposes of magic and prophecy, so to include it within your practice is natural.

The Havamal is from the Poetic Edda of the thirteenth century but perhaps composed earlier. If we look to *The Havamal*, the verse concerns those that shapeshift (the witch) and who fly at night.

Verses 147–165 of the Havamal are charms. Depending on which translation you follow, reciting the charm can cause either the hedge rider to show their true self and return home, or the rider's spirit to become separated from their physical body.

A tenth I know, what time I see
House-riders flying on high;
So can I work, that wildly they go,
Showing their true shapes,
Hence to their own homes.
Henry Adams Bellows (*Hovamol, verse 156*, The Poetic Edda, 1936)

The house/hedge riders fly to the otherworld to consult with spirits and gods for the purposes of magic or prophecy, often shape shifting.

Hedge riding, journeying, or visualizations can help to gain further advice from the spiritual world to use in the physical if the subject is not clear about what they want exactly, or the witch is having trouble determining what type of spell would work best.

Divination and Symbolism

As I say above in the section "Ingredients," do keep a journal to record journeys immediately after a riding or visualization for study and deciphering.

When hedge riding or journeying, or even when visualizing, messages and meanings often appear as symbols (not just spoken words and even they can be symbolic but also events without spoken words). Actual symbols such as runes or other forms of divination might be included in these. When using ridings for magical purposes the witch bears in mind the purpose for traveling. For instance, he or she might be working on a spell for decision making. Let us say this is to do with whether to move to a new house in another area. The spell is to help the petitioner see more clearly how such a move will affect them and perhaps their family. In traveling to the other realms, the witch will hope to discover more about the inner and outer truths of the matter. The witch can then create the spell more effectively.

Symbols and Messages

I have found divination, particularly the runes, helpful in "over the hedge" magic. I am sometimes given rune symbols as messages in the Otherworld, probably because I understand them. Otherworld spirit guides appear to work in a way that you will understand, just as spirit guides appear in forms that are comfortable to you.

I personally use runes, scrying, and tarot as divination methods in my witchcraft practice, and these often turn up in ridings. The runes though out of all of these, I use most often. They frequently appear in the Otherworld realms. Within a journey I may also scry into rivers, lakes, or bowls when they are presented to me seemingly for that purpose.

In my time as a witch, I have always included Norse and Celtic elements within my practice as I was drawn to them. I have recent Irish ancestry and resided in Ireland for many years. I also have Norwegian and Swedish ancestry. This might account for my natural leanings towards Celtic and Norse pantheons.

We have no control over what form messages might be delivered to us in ridings. But again, messages in symbol form often appear in forms you can understand or are at least able to decode.

As I mentioned above, messages often appear to me in the way of divination, though not always. I have had symbolic messages through a type of tree, such as birch or oak, or through the runes, or an archetypal figure that might be tarot related or through a guide's actions, animal, or spirit and where they take you. Occasionally I receive written messages. I am a great one for "sayings." These often come to mind during a rune reading or other form of divination and can summarize the core of the problem in a nutshell. One time I was taken up into the air by a golden eagle. I felt I was getting "a bird's eye view." I knew I was focusing too much on one small problem area and needed to "look at the bigger picture." This helped me put my problem into perspective.

If you hedge ride, you will already be familiar with journeying and what it entails. For the purposes of magic, go into the riding with the problem in mind. Ask for guidance. Take note of everything you see and write it down immediately you come out of the riding. There could be many events or symbols that stand out for you. Meanings might come to you while journeying or while "decoding" symbols and messages.

In this way hedge riding can be useful to help you decide the core of the problem and what type of spell to use. If the spell is for someone else, then do discuss this with them before making final decisions. A journey can also reveal to you what other elements you could add to your spell.

Hedge ridings can also help enhance a spell. Ask spirit guides for help getting your wishes out there in the universe.

Visualization

Not everyone is a hedge witch and hedge rides, however, you can get some benefit out of visualizations. Just as you can get to know your spell ingredients better as I describe in the section "Ingredients." You can look for symbols and messages. This works well when the spell is for you, as pathworking helps you get deeper into your unconscious and you occasionally "cross the hedge" too.

Think of the problem and choose a pathworking that is comfortable to you and you might enjoy: a walk on the beach, up a mountainside, along a country lane, on a boat on a river, or in the forest. Start the journey from home by opening a door and finding yourself in your chosen area. Return to the same door when you are ready.

Play soft unobtrusive meditation music, wear earplugs to cut out noise if necessary, such as traffic, light your candles and incense if you wish to enhance the atmosphere, and find a quiet moment when you can fully relax. Breathe steadily and relax every part of your body starting from your head. When you are fully relaxed, open the door. When you return give yourself a moment to come back to reality before recording everything you see. A journal is handy for this for future reference.

Hedge Riding Incense

To finish off I have included a recipe for incense. Grind in a mortar and pestle and burn on incense charcoal available from a magical supply shop. Use a mixture of any five of the following:

Bay
Catnip
Fennel
Frankincense resin
Lavender
Mugwort
Parsley
Poppy Seed
Sage
St John's Wort
Thyme

(For more on hedge riding please see my book in this series *Pagan Portals—Hedge Riding* also by Moon Books.)

A Note from Harmonia

Owing to the nature of the *Pagan Portal* series, this book is necessarily a short guide or introduction. I have not included many spells as the aim of the book is to provide you with a basic skill set and encourage you to create your own. However, there should be enough information in this book to give you a good start and plenty of ideas of how to move forward.

Good luck on your magical journey.

Harmonia Saille

Endnotes

1. Larner, Christine, *Witchcraft and Religion: The Politics of Popular Belief,* Basil Blackwell, Reprinted 1987 (P. 17)
2. Purkiss, Diane, *The Witch in History*, Routledge, Reprinted 1997 (P. 8)
3. Merrifield, Ralph. (Culemborg, The Netherlands.) "Witch Bottles and Magical Jugs." *Folklore Vol.66*, No.1, (March 1955). JSTOR
4. Purkiss, Diane, *The Witch in History*, Routledge, Reprinted 1997 (P. 134)

Bibliography

Andrews, Steve, *Herbs of the Northern Shaman*, O-Books, Hants, 2010

Becker, Udo, *The Continuum Encyclopedia of Symbols*, London, 2000

Bremness, Lesley (contributing editor), *Herbs*, Dorling Kindersley, New York/London, 1990

Crossley-Holland, Kevin, *Norse Myths: Gods of the Vikings*, Penguin Books Ltd, London, Reprinted 1993

Culpeper's Complete Herbal, Wordsworth Reference, 1995

Jung, Carl, G., (editor) *Man and His Symbols*, Aldus Books, London, Reprinted 1979

Jung, Carl, G., *Memories, Dreams, Reflections*, Vintage Books, 1989 edition

Larner, Christine, *Witchcraft and Religion: The Politics of Popular Belief*, Basil Blackwell, Oxford, Reprinted 1987

Nozedar, Adele, *The Element Encyclopedia of Secret Signs and Symbols*, Harper Element, London, 2008

Purkiss, Diane, *The Witch in History*, Routledge, London/New York, Reprinted 1997

Ravensky, Kimi, & Saille, Harmonia, *Crusty Crones Get Out and About*, Moon Books, Hants, 2011

Saille, Harmonia, *Pagan Portals – Hedge Witchcraft*, Moon Books, Hants, 2012

Saille, Harmonia, *The Spiritual Runes*, Moon Books, Hants, 2009

Saille, Harmonia, *Walking the Faery Pathway*, Dodona Books, Hants, 2009

Zalewski, C.L., *Herbs in Magic and Alchemy*, Prism Press, Dorset, Reprinted 1999

Suggested Reading

Patterson, Rachel, *Pagan Portals – Kitchen Witchcraft* (Moon Books, 2013)

Patterson, Rachel, *Pagan Portals – Moon Magic* (Moon Books, 2014)

Saille, Harmonia, *The Spiritual Runes* (Moon Books, 2009)

Saille, Harmonia, *Pagan Portals – Hedge Witchcraft* (Moon Books, 2012)

Saille, Harmonia, *Pagan Portals – Hedge Riding* (Moon Books, 2012)

Starza, Lucya, *Pagan Portals – Poppets and Magical Dolls* (Moon Books, 2018)

Starza, Lucya, *Pagan Portals – Candle Magic* (Moon Books, 2016)

Starza, Lucya, *Pagan Portals – Scrying* (Moon Books, 2022)

Other books by Harmonia Saille you might enjoy...

Hedge Witchcraft

Learning by experiencing is about trusting your instincts and connecting with your inner spirit

978-1-78099-333-1 (Paperback)
978-1-78099-330-0 (e-book)

Hedge Riding

The hedge is the symbolic boundary between the two worlds and this book will teach you how to cross that hedge

978-1-78099-348-5 (Paperback)
978-1-78099-349-2 (e-book)

**MOON
BOOKS**

PAGANISM & SHAMANISM

What is Paganism? A religion, a spirituality, an alternative
belief system, nature worship? You can find support for all these
definitions (and many more) in dictionaries, encyclopaedias, and
text books of religion, but subscribe to any one and the truth will
evade you. Above all Paganism is a creative pursuit, an encounter
with reality, an exploration of meaning and an expression of the
soul. Druids, Heathens, Wiccans and others, all contribute their
insights and literary riches to the Pagan tradition. Moon Books
invites you to begin or to deepen your own encounter, right here,
right now.
If you have enjoyed this book, why not tell other readers by
posting a review on your preferred book site.

Recent bestsellers from Moon Books are:

Journey to the Dark Goddess
How to Return to Your Soul
Jane Meredith
Discover the powerful secrets of the Dark Goddess and
transform your depression, grief and pain into healing
and integration.
Paperback: 978-1-84694-677-6 ebook: 978-1-78099-223-5

Shamanic Reiki
Expanded Ways of Working with Universal Life Force Energy
Llyn Roberts, Robert Levy
Shamanism and Reiki are each powerful ways of healing; together,
their power multiplies. *Shamanic Reiki* introduces techniques to
help healers and Reiki practitioners tap ancient healing wisdom.
Paperback: 978-1-84694-037-8 ebook: 978-1-84694-650-9

Pagan Portals – The Awen Alone
Walking the Path of the Solitary Druid
Joanna van der Hoeven
An introductory guide for the solitary Druid, *The Awen Alone* will
accompany you as you explore, and seek out your own place
within the natural world.
Paperback: 978-1-78279-547-6 ebook: 978-1-78279-546-9

A Kitchen Witch's World of Magical Herbs & Plants
Rachel Patterson
A journey into the magical world of herbs and plants, filled with
magical uses, folklore, history and practical magic. By popular
writer, blogger and kitchen witch, Tansy Firedragon.
Paperback: 978-1-78279-621-3 ebook: 978-1-78279-620-6

Medicine for the Soul
The Complete Book of Shamanic Healing
Ross Heaven
All you will ever need to know about shamanic healing and how to
become your own shaman...
Paperback: 978-1-78099-419-2 ebook: 978-1-78099-420-8

Shaman Pathways – The Druid Shaman
Exploring the Celtic Otherworld
Danu Forest
A practical guide to Celtic shamanism with exercises and
techniques as well as traditional lore for exploring the Celtic
Otherworld.
Paperback: 978-1-78099-615-8 ebook: 978-1-78099-616-5

Traditional Witchcraft for the Woods and Forests
A Witch's Guide to the Woodland with Guided Meditations and
Pathworking
Mélusine Draco
A Witch's guide to walking alone in the woods, with guided
meditations and pathworking.
Paperback: 978-1-84694-803-9 ebook: 978-1-84694-804-6

Wild Earth, Wild Soul
A Manual for an Ecstatic Culture
Bill Pfeiffer
Imagine a nature-based culture so alive and so connected,
spreading like wildfire. This book is the first flame...
Paperback: 978-1-78099-187-0 ebook: 978-1-78099-188-7

Naming the Goddess
Trevor Greenfield
Naming the Goddess is written by over eighty adherents and
scholars of Goddess and Goddess Spirituality.
Paperback: 978-1-78279-476-9 ebook: 978-1-78279-475-2

Shapeshifting into Higher Consciousness
Heal and Transform Yourself and Our World with Ancient
Shamanic and Modern Methods
Llyn Roberts
Ancient and modern methods that you can use every day to
transform yourself and make a positive difference in the world.
Paperback: 978-1-84694-843-5 ebook: 978-1-84694-844-2

Readers of ebooks can buy or view any of these bestsellers by
clicking on the live link in the title. Most titles are published in
paperback and as an ebook. Paperbacks are available in traditional
bookshops. Both print and ebook formats are available online.

Find more titles and sign up to our readers' newsletter at
http://www.johnhuntpublishing.com/paganism
Follow us on Facebook at https://www.facebook.com/MoonBooks
and Twitter at https://twitter.com/MoonBooksJHP